The
Wit and Wisdom
of the
Modern Ferrets

The
Wit and Wisdom
of the
Modern Ferrets

A Ferret's Perspective On Ferret Care

Edited by Mary R. Shefferman
Editor, *Modern Ferret* Magazine

Published by *Modern Ferret* Magazine

Notice of Liability
This book is designed to provide information in regard to pet ferret care. It is sold with the understanding that the publisher and author are not engaged in rendering veterinary advice. If veterinary assistance is required, the services of a competent professional should be sought.

It is not the purpose of this book to reprint all the information that is otherwise available to the author and/or publisher, but to complement, amplify, and supplement other texts. You are urged to read all the available material, learn as much as possible about ferrets, and to tailor the information to your individual needs.

Every effort has been made to make this book as complete and as accurate as possible. However, there may be mistakes both typographical and in content. Therefore, this text should be used only as a general guide and not as the ultimate source of ferret information. Furthermore, this book contains information on ferrets only up to the printing date.

The purpose of this book is to educate and entertain. The author and Modern Ferret shall have neither liability nor responsibility to any person or entity with respect to any loss or damage caused, or alleged to be caused, directly or indirectly by the information contained in this book.

If your ferret is ill, or you suspect your ferret is ill, you need to take your ferret to a ferret-knowledgeable veterinarian.

Trademarks
Throughout this book, trademarked names are used. Rather than put a trademark symbol in every occurrence of a trademarked name, we are using the names only in an editorial fashion and to the benefit of the trademark owner, with no intention of infringement of the trademark. Where those designations appear in this book, the designations have been printed in initial caps.

Manufactured in the United States of America
Library of Congress Card Number: 00-190387
ISBN 0-9667073-0-3

Publisher's Cataloging-in-Publication Data
Shefferman, Mary R.
　　　The Wit and Wisdom of the Modern Ferrets: A Ferret's Perspective On Ferret Care
　　　　　p.　　　　cm.
　　　"Tips and tricks to provide your ferret with better care and have more fun with your pet."
　　　Includes index.
　　　ISBN 0-9667073-0-3
　　　1. Ferrets as pets　　　　　I. Shefferman, Mary R. 1963-
　　　II. Title
　　　SF459.F47　　　　2000
　　　636.976628–dc20　　　　　00-190387

First Printing April 2000
10 9 8 7 6 5 4 3 2 1

Modern Ferret
PO Box 1007
Smithtown NY 11787

www.modernferret.com
www.ferretbooks.com

Choose Ralph.
Eat a crunchy. Sleep in a hammock.
Steal a sock. Miss a litterbox. Beg for a treat.
Poop in a corner. Knock something over.
But why would anyone want to do a thing like that?

Ralphspotting

Soon to be a major motion picture?

for Ralph

Mary and Balthazar

About the Editor

Mary R. Shefferman lives in New York with her husband, Eric, and their nine ferrets: Sabrina, Marshmallow, Knuks, Trixie, Bosco da Gama, Balthazar, Cauliflower, Koosh, and Gabrielle. Together, they publish *Modern Ferret* Magazine from their home.

Mary has a BA in English/Writing from Southampton College, Long Island University. She won the Readers and Writers of Southampton College Award for poetry in 1984 and 1985 and the John Steinbeck Award for poetry in 1984.

Before starting *Modern Ferret* Magazine in 1994, Mary was a managing editor and medical writer for Global Medical Communications in New York City.

Mary makes regular television appearances to promote proper ferret care on the Fox News Channel *Pet News*, MSG *Metro Pets*, and *The Family Pet*.

Mary is also the author of *The Ferret: An Owner's Guide to a Happy Healthy Pet*, published by Howell Book House in 1996.

CONTENTS

Introduction _____ 10

Sleeping Like a Log _____ 15

Safe Outlets _____ 17

Check for Lumps and Bumps _____ 18

"Nipper" in Napersville _____ 20

Secrets of the Litter Box _____ 22

Toys! _____ 24

Keep It Clean! _____ 26

Cheap Plastic Egg Toys _____ 27

Hold the Veggies, Please _____ 28

Don't Take Someone Else's Medicine _____ 30

The Couch Conquest _____ 32

Pants Legs! _____ 37

Home Sweet-Smelling Home
(or "Common Scents") _____ 38

Litter Box Moving _____ 40

Vaccinate! _____ 42

Winter Weight _____ 44

Boys Will Be Boys _____ 46

Styrofoam Is Dangerous! _____ 48

Bottle Brushes _____ 51

A Hair-Raising Experience _____ 52

Double-Check Prescriptions _____ 54

Safe Toys
(Hidden Dangers of Cardboard Tubes) _____ 56

Lend Me Your Ears _____ 57

Keep Your Ferret's Nails Trimmed _____ 58

The Radiator Incident _____60

Play It Safe! _____62

Shiver Me Timbers! _____64

Make an Isolation Cage _____66

Different Flavors! _____68

How's About A Kit? _____70

Climbing Mount Cageous _____73

Preventing Escapes_____76

Boys and Girls Get Along _____78

Bottle-Brush Tail _____80

Ferret-Proof! _____82

Cheap Toys! _____84

Marshmallow's Guide to Fine Dining
in Your Own Living Room _____86

Biting Electrical Cords_____89

Think Pink! _____90

The Fall Fashions _____92

Lapping Water From A Dish Is Fun! _____94

Ain't Misbehavin' _____96

Use a Pet Carrier
to Transport Your Ferret_____98

Rearranging the Litter Box_____ 100

Walk Like Me! _____ 103

The Trick of the Treat _____ 104

Be Nice To Ferrets
Who Can't See You _____ 106

Ferret Brushes! _____ 108

Taking Your Lumps... Off _____ 110

Find Out What Happened
(Post-Mortem Examinations) _____ 112

New Ferret Hazing &
Don't Like Baths _____ 114

Getting a Leg up With Humans _____ 116

Those Dangerous Holidays _____ 118

Extra Litter Boxes! _____ 122

The Scent of a Ferret (Hoo Ha!) _____ 124

How To Give Bad-Tasting Medicine _____ 126

Mortar and Pestle! _____ 127

Creative Thinking _____ 128

If You Can't Stand the Heat... _____ 130

Kao Lectrolyte
(Electrolyte Replenisher) _____ 132

The Litter Box Jitter Bug
(and related dance steps) _____ 134

Distracting Your Ferret
With Lickable Treats _____ 136

Don't Be Blue... It's Fur the Best _____ 138

Get a Second Medical Opinion _____ 140

If Ferrets Aren't Rodents,
Why Do They Get Rat Tail? _____ 142

Give a Kit a Smelly T-Shirt _____ 144

Appendix
Ten Tips For New Ferret Owners_____ 146

Checklist of Items
You'll Want to Have _____ 150

Index _____ 152

INTRODUCTION

OUR FIRST FERRET, SABRINA

Eric and I brought home our first ferret because of Arnold. Actually, it was Jerry, Arnold's ferret, who convinced me that a ferret could be a warm, cuddly pet. Before I met Jerry I held many of the common misconceptions about ferrets. But Eric had always wanted a ferret and he cleverly convinced Jerry to do his bidding. It worked.

In December of 1992 Eric and I went to pick out a ferret at the pet store where Arnold was working. There were two ferrets at the store, a baby ferret and a ferret someone had returned to the store after several months because they were bored with her. We were concerned that the older ferret might have a harder time than the baby ferret finding a home, so we chose her. We named her Sabrina. She was already litter trained and socialized. She showed us how well behaved and lovable ferrets could be. Sabrina is 8 years old now. She is still the most perfect little bundle of fur that anyone could want.

We had Sabrina for six months when we realized that she needed a friend. Eric and I were sometimes working long hours and we were concerned that Sabrina might be getting lonely. After meeting many adorable little ferrets, we chose Ralph. Ralph had markings that we had never seen before — he had a white stripe on his head. He was a most unique ferret. We later discovered that a ferret with Ralph's markings is called a "Blaze," so Ralph was not as unique as we had thought — color-wise, that is. Personality-wise Ralph was one in a million. He and

Sabrina ended up being good friends. As ferret owners know too well, once you adopt the mindset of adding "just one more" ferret, it can be very difficult to resist bringing home another. And another. Thus, over the years we have added quite a few to our business (a group of ferrets is called a "business").

How We Started *Modern Ferret* Magazine

When we brought home Sabrina, we also brought home some books on ferret care. Wanting to learn as much as we could about this new furry member of our family, we searched for more books about ferrets. We discovered that there weren't very many books and that the information in one sometimes conflicted with the information in another. It was around this time that Eric and I began to think about what we would like to do with our lives, what kind of work we'd like to be doing. We decided to combine our experience in publishing with our love for ferrets in creating a home-based business that would allow us to earn a living doing the things we enjoy. We would create the first magazine for ferret owners. After days of brainstorming, we came up with the name *Modern Ferret* for the magazine, and things started to fall into place.

About the Ferret Columns

One of the greatest challenges in magazine publishing is keeping the reader interested in the subject matter year after year. We have developed an entertaining way to present material that might otherwise become stale and repetitive — our ferrets have their own magazine columns. They write about various ferret-related topics from a ferret's perspective. All the ferret columns cover relevant and useful information, but they are presented in an inviting, fun-to-read fashion that makes learning about ferrets a pleasure. People bring ferrets into their lives for companionship and joy — we try to make learning how to care for them as enjoyable as living with them.

BACKGROUND INFORMATION

There are a few things you'll need to know in reading *The Wit and Wisdom of the Modern Ferrets*. This book is dedicated to Ralph. Ralph was the very first *Modern Ferret* columnist; he wrote a product review column called "Ralph's Reviews." After a very valiant battle against cancer, Ralph was put to rest in early September of 1998. He had lived far longer than anyone had expected, having been first diagnosed two years earlier. Ralph was possibly the most determined ferret I've ever encountered. He lived life with an enthusiasm that was inspirational. Ralph's dance of joy was the most joyous in our home. He loved to play and wouldn't give up on life until he absolutely had to. I think his last few months were a tribute to his sheer will to play and live every last moment. We chose not to include Ralph's columns in *The Wit and Wisdom*. We wanted to maintain an educational focus, and Ralph's product reviews didn't fit in with the editorial plan of the book. In addition, some of the products he reviewed are no longer available.

Knuks is deaf. Many ferrets with white fur on the head are deaf. Indeed, deafness and white fur/hair on the head are linked in other animals and humans as well. We've found that our two deaf ferrets (Ralph was also deaf) have been the most people oriented of our ferrets. It seems that many of the hearing ferrets would just as soon ignore us. Knuks makes some reference to her deafness in her columns, which, without knowing she is deaf, might be confusing to a new reader.

We have done very minimal editing to the columns and chose instead to add notations at the end of the columns to more fully cover the topic when necessary. These notes are in gray boxes. Several of the essays in this book cover topics that are seasonal in nature. Instead of editing the essays, we decided to leave in the seasonal references (e.g., to spring, the winter holidays).

ENJOY YOUR FERRETS

Ferrets are wonderful furry friends who bring great joy to our lives. *The Wit and Wisdom of the Modern Ferrets* serves as a guide to better understanding what goes on inside their furry little heads. The short chapters allow yout to take regular breaks to go play with your ferrets.

Ferrets are fun little bundles of mischief and play. By providing them with the care and attention they need, you can help them live happier and healthier lives. Enjoy them and enjoy the book.

Sincerely,

Mary R. Shefferman

Mary R. Shefferman
Editor, etc.

P.S. I have been told that ferrets can't talk. I know that. Our ferrets aren't *talking*, they're *writing*. Everyone knows ferrets can't talk.

Marshmallow Explains It All™

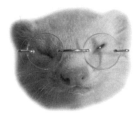

SLEEPING LIKE A LOG

Marshmallow has been a little difficult to live with these past few months. It seems he's a little envious of Ralph having his own column. So we talked it over and decided that Marshmallow could do a great service by explaining ferret behaviors to curious (and sometimes concerned) people. Let us know if you like it. And feel free to ask Marshmallow to explain any ferret behaviors you'd like to know more about.

***

I've been around ferrets all my life. I think that — plus the fact that I'm covered in fur and have a pointy nose — singularly qualifies me to talk about what we ferrets mean when we do certain things. So here goes.

Many of the ferrets I've spoken with have had this same experience when they were youngsters (kits, as you call them). They go to sleep — a nice deep wonderfully restful sleep — and before they know it some human is shaking them hysterically yelling, "Wake up!! You've got to wake up!!" Let's clear the air about this once and for all, shall we?

Relax, my large fur-less friends. Baby ferrets don't mean to frighten you when they go into their infamous deep, death-like sleeps. It's normal. Kits are either ON or OFF — they don't have a SLOW speed. When kits are in the off mode, they're really off. That way they'll have enough energy to go super-fast when they're awake. It's really quite simple.

I know what you're going to ask me: Why do ferrets act like this? The theory is that way back a few thousand years ago when we were (shudder) wild animals, we needed some way to protect the babies even when no one was there to keep watch over them. Seeing as most predators won't eat an animal that they find dead but not apparently killed by another animal, a baby ferret that *appears* dead is just as unappetizing as a really dead one. This is particularly true if the predator comes upon a whole nest of "dead" babies. A dead animal without wounds is a sign of disease, and many predators will not eat it.

So if your kit is sleeping like a log, let him! If you're really concerned, wake him *gently* by putting some food (or a favorite treat) under his nose. Please don't shake him up or make a sudden loud noise — that scares him. And you don't want to do that, do you? I thought not.

Until next time, this is Marshmallow, looking very smart in glasses.

This was the very first "Marshmallow Explains It All" column from *Modern Ferret* issue #8 in 1996. The title is a spoof of one of our favorite Nickelodeon shows "Clarissa Explains It All." It made a lasting change in the way ferrets talk about ferrets.

Nearly every ferret owner has been frightened at some time by a ferret who seemed to be dead but was actually just sleeping. Sabrina (our first ferret) played this trick on us just days after we brought her home. Sabrina was sleeping on Mary's lap when she suddenly sighed and seemed to stop breathing. After a few minutes of panic, we put some Ferretone in front of her nose and all of a sudden she started licking!

SAFE OUTLETS

Safe outlets aren't just for *human* children. Curious little ferrets can stick their noses into all sorts of things. You can use safety caps for your outlets to help prevent accidents.

Although a busybody ferret could remove one, it ought to give you time to notice what they're doing.

Safety caps are usually found by either baby items or electrical items. Treat your ferrets to some safety today!

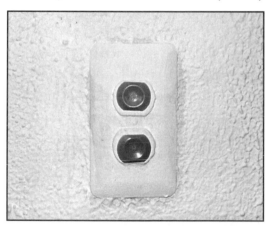

This was the first "Trixie's Tips" column, which appeared in *Modern Ferret* issue #15 in 1998. Although it took her a while to get started, Trixie has proven to be a very clever little girl with all sorts of useful tidbits of information.

Sabrina Says:™

CHECK FOR LUMPS AND BUMPS

It's always good practice to check for any strange bumps or lumps on or under your ferret's skin during the usual care and grooming routine. Ferrets can get skin tumors that can make them very itchy and can lead to more skin tumors. Even though these are usually benign, they need to be removed by your veterinarian. Your ferret could also get a cyst, which needs to be removed or lanced. While my humans were clipping my nails they discovered a bump on my toe that turned out to be a cyst. It didn't hurt or anything, but it wasn't very pretty. They took me to our veterinarian and he lanced the cyst. Lumps under the skin might mean that your ferret's lymph nodes are enlarged. Enlarged lymph nodes could indicate a serious problem. In either case, if you notice a lump or bump on your ferret, have your veterinarian take a look at it.

A good time to check your ferret for bumps is when you give him a bath, since you're rubbing him all over anyway. If you don't bathe your ferret very often (a lot of people don't), make a habit of checking your ferret for bumps whenever you clip nails or clean ears. Run your hands all over your ferret's body and feel for bumps or anything else abnormal — including cuts, scabs, or bald patches. A lot of ferrets like to be massaged all over. The better you know your ferret, the better you can take care of him by having your veterinarian check out potential problems right away. With many illnesses, recognizing the symptoms early can make a big difference.

Any skin tumor should be removed and biopsied because some tumors may be cancerous. Although mast cell tumors (a relatively common type) on the skin are most commonly benign, they do need to be removed. Mast cell tumors tend to spread; the longer they are left unchecked the more likely they are to spread.

Mast cell tumors can be very itchy, and a ferret may scratch at the tumor, causing scabbing and possibly leading to infection. Removing the tumor(s) will make your ferret much more comfortable.

See also "Taking Your Lumps... Off" on page 110.

Dear Gabby

YOUR ADVICE FERRET

"NIPPER" IN NAPERSVILLE

Dear Gabby:

I'm a young ferret and, though I'm ashamed to admit it, I sometimes play a little rough for my humans. I just get so worked up that I give them a little chomp. It's all in good fun, but they get real upset about it and say I'm being nippy. What is the best way they can teach me good manners without resorting to hurting me? I really do want to be good. It's just that I'm young and I don't think before I do something that I later regret.

— "Nipper" in Napersville

Dear Nipper:

Everybody — even your humans — was young once and *everybody* has made a mistake. It doesn't mean that you're bad, you just need to learn better manners. Everything is exciting and new to young ferrets, and in the process of being excited we can sometimes hurt the ones we love. Remember that you can play a lot rougher with your fellow ferrets than you can with your humans (the humans don't have the tough skin and fur that we have). As you get older, it will become easier for you to remember to be careful while you are playing.

One of the cleverest modern training techniques is the "timeout." Basically, all the equipment that's required is a small carrier (like what your parents should have for taking you on trips to the veterinarian). When you get too rambunctious, your parents can put you in the carrier for a few minutes until you calm down again. It is a wonderfully gentle way to teach you when you have done something "out of bounds." After a while, just the warning that you're going to get a "time-out" will be sufficient to help you remember to calm down and play gently.

Strike a pose!

Ferrets are individuals and different ferrets respond better or worse to different training methods. Baby ferrets, like other baby animals, explore their environment with their mouths (which they use as hands). Play fighting with their fellow ferrets teaches them how roughly they can play with each other. (You can hear when it gets too rough and one of the ferrets does the ferret version of "crying uncle.") You need to teach your ferret appropriate limits for playing with people.

Although there are several effective ways to train a ferret, the keys to success with any method are patience and consistency. A ferret that is frightened may take longer to train or, worse, may feel a need to defend himself by biting. Do not discipline a ferret out of anger, instead provide firm and consistent direction. Always praise good behavior.

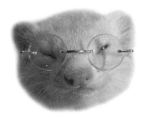

Marshmallow Explains It All™

SECRETS OF THE LITTER BOX

We ferrets must deal with a multitude of humiliations — from soapy baths and baby talk to over-adorable names and having our feces subject to daily inspection. Most of these we gladly tolerate in exchange for a treat. (Every ferret has his price.) Some of these perceived humiliations are for our own good.

Take daily stool inspections, for example. Our humans like to look at our feces, but for good reason. Because we ferrets have such a fast metabolism, the first place a sign of illness will often appear is the stool. Humans should always check litter boxes for any loose or odd-colored stools (black and tarry, green, or yellow), or if something in the stool looks out of place or unusual (foreign body). If there is more than one of these odd stool specimens, a trip to the veterinarian is most likely in order. (Don't forget to bring along the stool for the veterinarian to examine.) If there are two or more loose stools in a row (diarrhea), your ferret needs to see a veterinarian right away, *before* he becomes dehydrated. If you have more than one ferret using a particular litter box, a separate cage for isolating the potentially ill ferret will be helpful.

Foreign bodies in the stool should be of *great* concern to humans, since intestinal blockage can lead to death very quickly. You need to determine where the foreign object came from and whether the ferret passed the entire object. If you suspect there's something still in your ferret, take him to the veterinarian. A ferret with loose stools along with vomiting or refusal to eat needs *immediate* veterinary attention.

During shedding seasons, a stool that contains clumps of fur is a sign that your ferret needs a hairball remedy to make sure he continues to pass the fur. Ferrets have experienced partial intestinal obstructions caused by swallowed fur.

For the most part, a single loose or odd-colored stool may be observed from time to time. Sometimes we ferrets eat something that doesn't agree with us (a bug, for example). Humans should become concerned by a further observation of unusual feces.

Humans can learn a lot about us ferrets by making a quick survey of the contents of the litter box when removing the feces each day. If something is amiss, keep your eyes open for other signs of illness and act accordingly. Remember, we can't take ourselves to the veterinarian; we don't see well enough to drive.

We can't stress enough that observing your ferret's behavior (eating, drinking, litter box, energy level, attitude, etc.) and watching for unusual changes is the best way to catch medical problems early and keep your ferret healthy.

See also "Ain't Misbehavin'" on page 96.

Sabrina Says:™

Toys!

Our humans brought us home a couple of neat playthings: miniature laundry baskets (they're also called organizer baskets). Our humans got them at an office supply store, but I think you can get them at other types of stores, too. The baskets come in several different sizes, colors, and shapes. In addition to rectangular ones and round ones, there are even ones shaped like a heart.

These baskets are usually pretty sturdy, though some are made of a harder plastic than others. If you have ferrets that chew on plastic, these might not work for you; or you will need the sturdier variety of basket. Also, don't get the baskets that have larger holes (or slots) for handles; your ferret could get his head stuck!

We ferrets really enjoy playing in the baskets. Ralph especially likes to lie down in them when he gets sleepy — sometimes he even puts some of his toys in the basket with him. Ralph, Marshmallow, and Knuks all like to wrestle with a jingle ball while they're in the basket — that way if the ball gets away from them, they don't have to get up and chase after it.

Not all of us ferrets like to lie down or play in the basket (I prefer hammocks). But almost every one of us likes to climb in and out of them. Sometimes a big ferret (like Bosco) tips over the baskets, creating a little wall, and then we use them as a place to hide things.

Humans can use the baskets, too. When your ferrets are finished playing and have gone to sleep, you can take all their toys from where they belong and put them into the baskets. Sort of like a child's toy box. Then, the next time your ferrets come out to play, they'll have to put all the toys back where they're supposed to be (like under the TV stand). It's OK, we know that a ferret's work is never done.

Like any toy your ferrets play with, you should make sure no one is chewing it. If your ferrets chew the basket, try a harder plastic basket. If they still chew it, you may not be able to use one of these baskets as a toy for your ferrets. Remember that safety always comes first — even if it means we can't have a neat plaything.

Ralph loves to belly-slide into the baskets!

My tips!

Trixie's Tips™

KEEP IT CLEAN!

Healthy, well-groomed ferrets shouldn't stink. One way to help reduce any odors is to wash your ferret's blankets, hammocks, and sleep sacks at least once a week (more frequently if you have more ferrets). Ferrets tend to emit a warm, mild musky scent when they're sleeping. But as that pleasant, mild scent builds up in fabrics it can become much stronger — and much less pleasant. As your ferret sleeps in smelly blankets, he can pick up a stronger aroma himself. Remember that bathing your ferret too often can cause him to overproduce skin oils to compensate for the drying effect of some shampoos, thus making him work up a scent more quickly. Sometimes you may find that changing the blankets works just as well as bathing your ferret. Also periodically clean any climbing/tunneling toys.

Feeding a good food, keeping litter boxes clean, and keeping your ferret's ears clean can all help to reduce any odors as well.

If you choose to use one of the new odor elimination products (e.g., Febreze), note that the ASPCA National Animal Poison Control Center recommends that you use the product exactly as indicated in the directions. If the product needs to dry completely before it is safe, make sure to follow those instructions.

Sabrina Says:™

CHEAP PLASTIC EGG TOYS

A very special kind of toy that you can usually find very cheaply this time of year is the plastic egg. Some ferrets like to push them with their noses, some like to sit on them and push them back into a corner, and some just like to pick up the egg halves and carry them to a special hiding place.

In any case, the eggs are generally made of hard plastic which won't break with rough ferret play and chewing. However, you should always watch the toys your ferret is playing with for signs of breakage or danger to your ferret.

Some large ferrets can crush the smaller eggs in their mouths. Always supervise your ferret's interactions with toys and take away toys that are not safe or that become damaged. Remember that every ferret is unique and plays with his toys differently. Some ferrets are more interested in eggs of different sizes (e.g., Koosh loves to play with very large plastic eggs but smaller ones do not interest him at all).

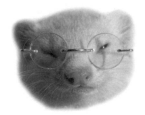

Marshmallow Explains It All™

HOLD THE VEGGIES, PLEASE

Ferrets belong to the order *Carnivora*, thus we are referred to as "carnivores." This means that we eat meat (Webster prefers the phrase "flesh-eating," which I find a bit ghoulish). Herbivores eat plants. Omnivores eat anything they can get their lips around. Much as ferrets like the occasional raisin or melon, we are not omnivores. And we are certainly not herbivores. We need the nutrients in meat to survive and thrive.

Some people are under the mistaken impression that protein is protein. To humans, yes, it is. But we are not humans (thank the Lord for small favors). A human's body can extract the protein from grains as well as that from meats. A ferret's body cannot. Although we are superior to many animals (including humans at times) in many ways, this is one area in which we sadly come up short. You see, we do not have an area in our intestines called a caecum (or cecum). This is a pouch at the beginning of the large intestine where plant materials are digested. It's a sort of layover area, because plant material is more complex and takes longer to break down than animal material/meat.

But ferrets don't have that sort of time. Ferrets have only three to four hours to fully digest their food and get the nutrients they need from it. So, it isn't that there isn't *enough* protein in plants or that it's the wrong kind, it's that we ferrets can't get the protein out of the plants in the time we have to digest them. Animal protein is far more accessible than plant protein.

Overall, ferrets are built to eat meat. Aside from our lacking a caecum, our teeth are made to tear food, not grind it. The range of motion of our jaws is up and down, not side to side. That's one of the reasons you see ferrets tilting their heads in the course of eating — it's to move the food to a spot where it can be crushed. (Another reason for chewing on one side of the mouth is a bad tooth — humans should certainly rule out this possibility if their ferret suddenly begins to chew in an unusual manner.)

Besides, we *like* meat. Of course, many ferrets do also like some fruits and vegetables, but these should be given only as treats. The mainstay of our diets must be our regular food — formulated for us, the little carnivores.

When we started *Modern Ferret* in 1994, there were few high-quality ferret foods available. Most ferret owners fed high-quality (high meat protein) kitten foods. As the popularity of ferrets has increased, the demand for better foods has led several manufacturers to make ferret foods that meet or exceed a ferret's nutritional needs. Remember to always look for foods that have meat as the first (main) ingredient(s).

Sabrina Says:™

DON'T TAKE SOMEONE ELSE'S MEDICINE

Almost everyone knows that it's a bad idea to take another person's medication, but that doesn't stop some people from giving their ferret medication that their vet didn't prescribe for the ferret. You should not give your ferret medications that your vet prescribed for another animal in your home, whether it's a dog, cat, or another ferret — even if the ferret seems to have the same or similar symptoms. Ferrets need different dosages of medicines from other animals, and even different ferrets might need different dosages if they are different sizes. You should *always* check with your veterinarian before giving your ferret medicine.

It's also not a good idea to give your ferret human medicines. Some human medications can be very harmful to your ferret, even if they're safe for you. Even though most ferrets think they're people (and a lot of people think ferrets are people, too), that doesn't mean we are. Besides, a ferret is very tiny compared to a human, so even if the medicine is OK for the ferret, the amount you have to give him will be very different. If you can't get in touch with your veterinarian, make sure you have a phone number for an emergency veterinarian.

If you or someone in your house has given a ferret medication that you're not sure about or if the ferret has gotten into medication that he shouldn't have (or you're not sure if he should have it), contact the Animal Poison Control Center. This is a non-profit organization that has 24-hour service provided by veterinarians. Try to find out what the medication was and how much your ferret ate. You will also have to tell them the age of your ferret, how much he or she weighs, and if he or she has some other illness. It's important to stay as calm as possible and listen carefully so you can give the veterinarian the right information to help your ferret. The phone numbers are:

900-680-0000 ($20.00 for the first five (5) minutes plus $2.95 for each additional minute)

800-548-2423 ($30.00 per case, payable by credit card)

Normal weight can vary greatly from one ferret to another (our lightest, Knuks, is less than a pound, while our heaviest, Cauliflower, is approximately 5 pounds) and from season to season (our Ralph was often 2 pounds in the summer and 3 pounds in the winter). Dosages for many medicines for ferrets are based on body weight; therefore, what might be appropriate for one ferret might be too much or too little for another.

THE COUCH CONQUEST

One of my duties as a ferret is to keep my humans on their toes. Let me tell you, it's a thankless task, but someone has to do it. I have been called "naughty," "annoying," and "pesty." In fact, my humans often refer to me as "The Pest."

Pestiness is not so much a routine you learn as it is an art you develop. I would like to help my fellow ferrets improve their art, so I'm here to offer a little direction in how to be pesty.

This first lesson is called: "How To Be Pesty in the Living Room Furniture," or "Breaking and Entering the Couch." Many ferrets are quite accomplished at getting into couches. Humans tend to dislike this for some reason. But we know that inside a couch is the best place to hide, sleep, and poop. It's like a big, dark house. Owners go on about stuffing and foam and getting squashed (believe me, I've been subjected to the lectures over and over again — lucky for me I can't hear and the humans can't tell that I'm not reading their lips).

There are several methods for entering the couch. The "through-the-top" method works for many ferrets. Simply push aside the cushion and scratch incessantly at the fabric underneath until you make a hole. You're in. Piece of cake.

The "under-the-bottom" method is met with equal amounts of success as the upper entry method. Go under the couch, lie on your back, and scratch incessantly at the fabric until you make a hole. You're in. More cake.

Ferrets with humans that are too smart for their own good might have to face the Futon Challenge. Futons are these terrible human sitting devices that have no insides. But they do have a giant cushion on them which can be penetrated using the incessant scratching technique. If you do not have your incessant scratching technique down pat, you'll never see the inside of the furniture. Practice makes perfect (and irritates humans in a very amusing way).

There are also special case couches, like the one I broke into. The humans took for granted that no ferret could get into the couch. Sabrina, Ralph, and Marshmallow had not managed to get into the couch (and they call themselves ferrets!). But nothing is Pest-Proof! I was inside before our very first play session in the new house was over.

Here's how I did it. First, I discovered an opening in the couch's defense: an exposed area of some weird web-like fabric between the couch's frame and its base. Because the base of the couch rested on the floor and there was no obvious access to the underside (or inside) of the couch, the humans thought it was an impenetrable fortress. I located the easily shredded fabric and I used the incessant scratching technique to tear a small hole in it. I was in. It was glorious!

Then the humans found out what I did. They picked up the couch, cut a slit in the bottom, and forcibly removed me from my cozy paradise. I was furious, and I let them know it (another key part to being a pest is having elaborate tantrums). Then, as if that wasn't enough, they sealed up the entrance to the couch. This presents even more of a challenge, but I'm up for it. I won't let them rest until I get into that couch again. One of the ways I don't let them rest is I use the versatile incessant scratching technique on their pants legs whenever they sit on the couch. If they pick me up, I squirm until they put me on the couch so I can explore other points of entry. Unfortunately, the humans seem to be onto my plot and keep putting me back on the floor.

I'll keep you posted on how the couch conquest progresses. In the meantime, practice your pestiness!

Ferret-Proofing
Our Ferret-Proof Couch

by Mary R. Shefferman

If there's one rule with ferret-proofing, it is this: There are no rules.

When we brought home our first ferret (Sabrina) we were living in a fairly large house that had room for a pair of matching couches. The couches are constructed like a platform bed: the wooden couch frame (covered in foam and fabric) is attached on a wooden base (covered with fabric). The wooden base is flush with the floor, so there is no way a ferret (or anything) could get under the couch by going under the base.

Sabrina used to scratch at the base of the couches, but she never made a hole. Even if she had made a hole in the fabric covering the base, she wouldn't have been able to get inside the couch. Ralph and Marshmallow also never got inside the couches. Because of this, we assumed the couches were ferret safe.

When we moved to a smaller place, the couches went into storage. During this time, we brought home the rest of the ferrets: Knuks, Trixie, Bosco, and Balthazar. Now that we've moved into a larger place again, we brought our presumably ferret-safe couches with us.

To our surprise and dismay, on the very first night with the ferrets in our new home, Knuks got inside one of the couches. We had to slit the bottom of the couch to get her out (since she's deaf, we couldn't use a squeak toy to lure her out). We surveyed the situation. We discovered a gap between the frame and the base of the couch; that is, the base is smaller than the frame. The gap is covered only by a thin web-like couch-bottom fabric. It's just large enough (ranging from 1.5 to 2 inches) for the tiny Knuks to get inside.

The hole Knuks made to get in.

Cutting small pieces of wood and nailing them on to cover the gap.

Since both the frame and base of the couch are wood, we figured wood would be the best material to use to seal the gap. We considered fabric, but knowing that Knuks was (is) determined to get back into the couch, we figured

Now the hole is covered by something tougher than cloth.

she'd eventually scratch through any fabric we used.

First we measured the entire perimeter of the couch. Then we went to a lumber store and bought enough 2-inch wide molding to go around both couches. The couches have three straight edges and one curved. The most challenging part was covering the gap around the rounded end of the couch. We cut the wood into 3-inch strips and nailed the small pieces around the curve. The straightaways were easy to seal up. We used a lot of 1-inch nails to ensure that the wood strips would not come off. The actual nailing down of the wood went very quickly.

When we flipped the couches right-side-up, we discovered that the wood strips were partially visible, but since it is consistent around the entire couch on both couches, we figured most people wouldn't even notice. Besides, we'd rather have a safe couch than a pretty couch.

So far, there's been some scratching at the wood, but no ferrets inside the couch. Knuks is not very amused.

We covered the gap all around the base of the couch so that the ferrets wouldn't be able to find any other weak spots. Although it doesn't look 100% professional, very few people look at the underside of our couch!

Trixie's Tips™

My tips!

PANTS LEGS!

Ferrets love tubes and tunnels, so why not give 'em what they want? If you have some old pairs of pants, you can make a great tube for your ferrets to play in. Our humans took old jeans that were ripped or that had broken zippers and they cut off the legs. Then they gave us the legs to play in. We love to crawl through them and chase each other through them. You can also use sweatpants or other types of pants or you can use long sleeves off sweatshirts. Just make sure that the fabric is kind of sturdy and that no ferrets can catch a nail on it. Some of us even go to sleep in the pants leg tubes. If you have a ferret who's a "cloth chewer," try spraying the ends of the tube with Bitter Apple or some other chewing deterrent before giving it to the ferrets. As with any toys, take them away if they show signs of wear or if someone is chewing on them.

It's tunnelin' time!

Marshmallow Explains It All™

HOME SWEET-SMELLING HOME (OR "COMMON SCENTS")

The ferret nose is a highly sophisticated, delicately calibrated, and powerful instrument. It can detect scents far more readily and accurately than the primitive human olfactory senses. Therefore, I was taken aback when I discovered that our humans had taken into consideration the ferret's sense of smell when preparing a new playhouse for us ferrets. One would expect humans to overlook the obvious method for deterring less civilized ferrets from using the playhouse as a latrine — making it smell like a sleeping spot. For round-headed animals, our humans sometimes display a surprisingly high level of intelligence.

Ferrets mark their various living areas (e.g., sleep, toilet, play) with specific and complex scents. We use our most relied-upon sense — smell — to navigate our world in light or in darkness. This is how, for example, even though Sabrina can no longer see, she still finds the litter box, hammock, and food without fail.

Our humans took blankets from one of our sleeping areas and placed them inside the playhouse. When we entered the playhouse to investigate, we were greeted with a familiar smell. Not only was it a smell we all recognized, but it was a clear signal that this was a sleeping/playing area and not a place to leave waste material. We exceptionally evolved ferrets certainly appreciated the help in keeping the more barbaric members of our business from inappropriately soiling this wonderful den. Now we all get to sleep and snuggle in the comforting darkness of the playhouse, which pleases me to no end.

Humans, take note: It is often a good idea to mark with smells the various areas you wish your ferret to use for the various activities he must perform (i.e., toilet, sleep, food, play). Of course, there are ferrets like myself who don't require such olfactory landmarks to figure out what to do in a litter box or in a playhouse: we know quite well what's what and what it's for.

So the next time you need to inform your ferret what you would like him to do and where you would like him to do it, try thinking smart, like a ferret. Communicate with him in a language he understands instead of that gibberish you humans usually use. Soon your home will smell just right too.

If your ferrets use an inappropriate spot for a bathroom, it is very important that you remove trace odors from the area because those trace odors help mark bathroom locations. There are several enzyme-based odor removal products available at pet stores to help you remove all traces of bad odors. Use these products according to label directions.

Sabrina Says:™

LITTER BOX MOVING

Litter box moving is a favorite sport among many ferrets. In most cases, it is harmless. But other times, the ferrets might dump out the contents of the litter box, creating a mess. Owners tend to disapprove of such activity. Especially since they are the ones who have to clean up the mess.

If the bottom of the ferret's cage is flat (not wire mesh), there is a solution — Velcro. All you have to do is use the Velcro to firmly attach the litter box to the bottom of the cage. It doesn't even take a lot of Velcro to make the litter box into an immovable object. Here's how:

1

Cut off two 4-inch lengths of the loop part and two 4-inch lengths of the fuzzy part of the Velcro, and attach the loop parts to the fuzzy parts. Make sure the inside bottom of the cage and the bottom of litter box are clean.

2

Remove the paper backing from the loop side of the Velcro and stick the Velcro onto the short end of the bottom of the litter box. Do the same with the other length of Velcro.

3

Remove the remaining paper backing so the bottom of the litter box has two exposed sticky sides. Stick the litter box onto the bottom of the cage in the place where you want it to stay. Press firmly so the adhesive sticks to the cage bottom.

4

Pull up on the litter box. Now the two strips of fuzzy Velcro should be stuck to the inside bottom of the cage and the two loop strips should be stuck to the bottom of the litter box — and they should line up perfectly.

If your ferret can still move the litter box, add two more 4-inch strips of Velcro on each side of the bottom of the litter box (so all four sides have Velcro strips). If your ferret can still move the litter box, you need to get the concrete model!

Thanks to Nina Trischitta of Lindenhurst, NY, for this great tip!

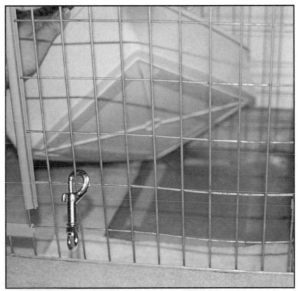

Note the clip lock hanging by the cage door. We use these clips to lock swinging cage doors closed as an extra security measure so that ferrets can't force their way out (or worse, force their way halfway out and get stuck).

My tips!

Trixie's Tips™

VACCINATE!

Ferrets need two kinds of shots. They need to get a canine distemper shot so they don't get canine distemper. Canine distemper is a really bad virus and ferrets who get it die (there is no cure). When ferrets are babies, they need a distemper shot when they're 6 to 8 weeks old, 10 to 12 weeks old, and 13 to 14 weeks old (the last shot has to be at or after 14 weeks). After that, they get a canine distemper shot once a year.

Ferrets also need a rabies shot. They can get their first rabies shot when they are 12 weeks (3 months) old. Then they get a shot once a year after that.

It's really important to make sure your ferret stays current with his shots. You wouldn't want him to get sick or die because he didn't get a shot. Canine distemper is an airborne virus and, even if your ferret doesn't go outside, you or other pets in your house can bring it in the house and infect him. That would be terrible!

The rabies shot is really important too. If your ferret bites or scratches someone — even by mistake — and he has had his rabies shot, the authorities will probably just quarantine him (check with your local authorities, because this can be different in different places). But if your ferret doesn't have his rabies shot, the authorities might want to test him to see if he has rabies, and they have to kill a ferret to test him for that!

Your vet should use USDA-approved vaccines for your ferret — Fervac-D (canine distemper) and Imrab-3 (rabies). Always wait at your vet's office for at least 30 minutes after your ferret gets a shot just in case he has a reaction to the shot. Also keep an eye on your ferret for the next 24 hours. If your ferret has had a reaction to a shot, talk with your vet about how to handle shots in the future.

Keep your fuzzies safe and healthy — vaccinate them!

Any animal (or human) can experience a reaction to a vaccine. To help reduce the chance of a reaction, many veterinarians (and the vaccine manufacturers) recommend waiting two weeks between the rabies and the canine distemper shots. Make sure your ferret is healthy when he goes for each vaccination. Your veterinarian will give him a checkup before the shot, but if you've noticed any odd behavior or diarrhea or vomiting in the days prior to the vaccination appointment, tell your veterinarian. He may want to postpone the shot until your ferret is 100%. After the vaccination, wait at the veterinarian's office for at least 30 minutes. Check on your ferret frequently during this time. If your ferret paws at his mouth, vomits, has diarrhea or bloody stools, or loses consciousness, notify the veterinarian immediately (don't worry about barging in!). Since vaccine reactions can occur even hours later, keep an eye on your ferret for 24 hours. (Our Balthazar had a mild reaction after a recent vaccination. Eight hours after his vaccination, he started vomiting. A trip to the emergency veterinary clinic for treatment got him feeling better quickly.) Although the possibility of vaccine reactions is scary, the consequences of not vaccinating your ferret are scarier. Canine distemper is virtually 100% fatal for ferrets and rabies is also fatal. Overall, the benefits of vaccinating your ferret outweigh the risk of a reaction, except in cases of severe prior reactions.

Dear Gabby

YOUR ADVICE FERRET

WINTER WEIGHT

Dear Gabby:

Winter is coming and I'm starting to lose my girlish figure. I mean I'm really porking out! What should I do?

— Hefty in Hooterville

Dear Hefty:

You can't fight Mother Nature! Ferrets can undergo dramatic weight gains for winter and dramatic weight

I'm chunky, but I'm plush!

losses for summer. It's in our nature. Some of the ferrets here at *Modern Ferret* have summer weights of 2 pounds and winter weights of over 3 pounds. Ferrets recognize changes in the cycle of day and night and "know" when it is time to change for the next season. These changes also include changing coats, which can sometimes lead to dramatic color changes as well.

Ferrets are born thinking that it is summer and that their first seasonal change should be to put on winter weight and a winter coat. However, many ferrets in pet stores were bred on breeding cycles that don't match the natural seasons (which is why pet stores have baby ferrets year-round). That means that the ferrets can start putting on winter weight and a winter coat at the wrong time (the photo of me was taken in July). They then can start to lose their winter coat and winter weight just as winter is really setting in. Sometimes it can take several years of being around natural lighting for a ferret to readjust to proper seasonal changes. Sometimes the artificial lighting situations in people's homes (not being exposed to full natural daylight cycles) can also fool ferrets into acting like it is the wrong season.

Of course, weight changes that seem too drastic or don't appear to be seasonal should always be checked out by a veterinarian. Especially if they are accompanied by lethargy, lack of appetite, vomiting, yukky poops, lack of poops, or other signs of the ferret not being well.

Hey folks! Write to me! I love getting letters! I make a big pile of them and stand on top of them. When the pile gets high enough, it topples over and I ride the avalanche of envelopes like a cool surfer-chick! It's FUN! So keep those letters coming!

Dear Gabby

YOUR ADVICE FERRET

Go for the logo!

Marshmallow Explains It All™

BOYS WILL BE BOYS

As an expert ferret, I am often called upon to dispel myths and correct misinformation regarding my species. I appreciate these opportunities to educate the less enlightened; I feel it is my responsibility to share my knowledge with others. I believe I must speak out against misrepresentation and falsehoods. For if I do not stand up for my furry brethren, who will?

It is with this purpose that I now address a half-truth that was recently brought to my attention. There are some humans who are under the false impression that boy ferrets cannot get along with each other under any circumstances. Of course we can! In fact, some of my dearest friends are boys: Ralph, Bosco da Gama, and Balthazar. We all get along splendidly. Here's why: we have all been neutered. Had our anatomical parts been left intact, we might not get along quite as well as we do, particularly during the mating season. Intact males do tend to become territorial during that time of year, often fighting in earnest and are even capable of killing each other. Therefore, intact males should not be housed together when they are in season. The rest of us are more commonly relaxed about those ferrets with whom we associate. In short, once the sex hormones are removed, very few disagreements can bring us to serious blows.

A related myth is that male ferrets in season are more aggressive toward humans than during other times of the year. No. They are more aggressive to other male ferrets. On some occasions a male ferret in season might be less than friendly with a human, but the main brunt of their aggression is directed at "the competition," that is, other male ferrets.

I am hopeful that this short essay will help to eradicate the misconception that boy ferrets cannot get along with one another. With that, I shall go curl up with my dear friend Ralph.

Pet ferrets should be neutered — both males (castration) and females (spay). Neutering helps them to be better pets. Sexually intact male ferrets can give off a strong unpleasant odor when they go into season (rut). Sexually intact female ferrets can get very ill if they go into season (estrus) and are not bred. A female ferret that is not brought out of estrus can develop a life-threatening form of anemia. Only breeding or a hormone shot from a veterinarian will bring the ferret out of estrus. Most ferrets that come from pet stores are neutered before they leave the breeder farm, so neutering is not a concern for most ferret owners.

Once ferrets are neutered there is usually no problem integrating them into one group. Of course, ferrets are individuals and occasionally two ferrets may not get along. Time, patience, and gradual introductions are the keys to helping ferrets learn to like each other.

Sabrina Says:™

STYROFOAM IS DANGEROUS!

Ferrets can get intestinal blockages very easily by swallowing things that they can't pass through their narrow intestines. How narrow are ferret intestines? Take the ink cartridge out of a Bic Stic pen and look at the empty barrel. That's about how narrow ferret intestines are. Usually blockages are caused by something that ferrets like to chew on, like foam rubber, latex, or Styrofoam. Your ferret's digestive tract cannot break down these substances.

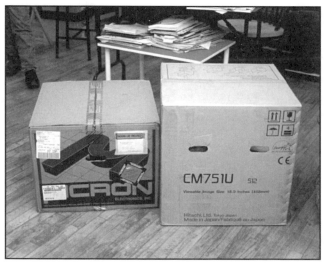

Our new 266 MHz Pentium Machine from Micron —
now we're really going to do some great stuff!

Most people realize that Styrofoam "peanuts" pose a danger to their ferrets, but don't think about other forms of Styrofoam. You wouldn't think so, but even blocks of Styrofoam can "shed" little pieces that can scatter around your room. This creates a hazard that not everyone readily notices. Even Styrofoam-like packing material made from potato is not really safe for ferrets because the potatoes are not food grade. Let's face it: eating Styrofoam of any sort is just not good for ferrets. As a ferret owner, it's your job to keep dangerous things like these away from your ferrets.

Recently, a couple of big boxes were delivered to our house. These boxes had Styrofoam inside them to help protect the expensive items that were packed in the boxes. A lot of boxes come with Styrofoam inside to protect the contents: TVs, toasters, computers, even ready-to-assemble furniture. It is very important that people be aware of the packing materials from their new appliances and such. The best thing to do is unpack boxes in areas that are always off-limits to your ferrets. If you can't do

Note the Styrofoam breaking off and making little pieces.

that, remember to clean up (vacuum) after opening packages. Make sure you vacuum the *whole room*, not just the area where the box was opened.

Why do you need to vacuum the whole room? Sometimes Styrofoam can get statically charged and stick onto the floor or carpeting (or your clothing). Don't take any chances with this: sweeping may not be enough to pick up this "sticky" Styrofoam. Also, because Styrofoam is so light, pieces of it can easily float across the room. Vacuuming thoroughly will pick up all of these potentially dangerous pieces. Also check your clothes after you've handled Styrofoam packing to make sure you haven't become a hazard yourself!

When you have ferrets, you have to constantly be thinking about what they can get into or what they might eat by mistake. A lot of people don't even realize that something as silly as Styrofoam packing can be a danger to their ferrets. When you bring home a new TV or computer you don't want the pleasant experience of getting new stuff to be overshadowed by a trip to the veterinarian with a ferret whose intestines are blocked. And your ferret certainly doesn't want to have to go through a surgery that could have been avoided.

Keep your eyes open and your mind on the alert for potential dangers to your ferret. Being careful pays off.

Trixie's Tips™

My tips!

BOTTLE BRUSHES

Ferret water bottles can become kind of unsanitary if they aren't cleaned properly. Algae can grow in the bottle (yuck!). To prevent icky water bottles, make sure you clean them thoroughly with hot sudsy water. To really get the bottle clean, scrub the inside with a bottle brush. (Not a scared-y ferret's tail, silly! See the photo!) You can find bottle brushes in the baby products aisle of the supermarket or at a drug store — or any store that carries items for babies. They are inexpensive, but they can help you keep your ferret's drinking water clean and fresh. Believe me, ferrets appreciate that.

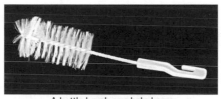

A bottle brush can help keep your ferret happy and healthy.

Even with routine cleaning, water bottles can deteriorate. You should replace all water bottles periodically.

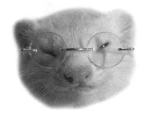

Marshmallow Explains It All™

A HAIR-RAISING EXPERIENCE

Lest you think I am the uncommon exception among ferrets, let me state at the outset that there is none more typical than I. I am susceptible to the same misfortunes as any other ferret. I groom my fur one leg at a time, just like everybody else.

It is the unfortunate consequence of this grooming which I shall discuss in this column. Despite the best efforts of my humans, I found myself suffering from the dreadful discomfort of hairballs in my stomach. Before you torment yourselves regarding your own best efforts (O! Imperfect Homosapiens!), note that ferrets are by their nature a bit weaselly and are exquisitely equipped to outsmart even the most learned human. Frequently I surreptitiously aided other ferrets in their grooming regimens; my humans erroneously believed that if I was not personally shedding then I did not require administration of a hairball remedy to help the loose fur pass through my delicate digestive tract. Humans take note: When one sheds, hairball remedy for all.

Several months ago, I began to have intermittent diarrhea (the horror!). I even vomited once or twice. My humans took me to the veterinarian, who prescribed antibiotics. My condition improved while I was taking the medication, but soon after I finished the full course of the antibiotic treatment I began to show symptoms again. At this juncture, an x-ray was taken which indicated that there was indeed "something" in my stomach that required removal. My veterinarian performed the surgery, removing two reasonably sized hairballs from my stomach. Suffice it to say that my stomach was not itself for some time after.

If you should observe in your ferret symptoms of a partial intestinal blockage, bring him to your veterinarian. The following signs are indicative of partial blockage: intermittent diarrhea or poorly formed, narrow stools; vomiting — even once or twice; a change in eating behavior (a tendency to eat smaller meals or refuse treats). All ferrets groom themselves and other ferrets; therefore, all ferrets are susceptible to a partial intestinal blockage caused by hairballs — regardless of whether they have a propensity for swallowing foreign objects. Observe your ferrets keenly and act when action is required.

I leave you with this bit of wisdom: It is far better to keep your hairballs in a vial on the mantle than to keep them in your stomach.

If your ferret has insulinoma and has to have his sugar intake restricted, talk with your veterinarian about using plain petroleum jelly (the active ingredient in hairball remedies) instead of commercially available hairball remedies, which contain various forms of sugar. The following ingredients are all forms of sugar (which helps make the hairball remedy more palatable): malt syrup, malt extract, molasses, etc.

Note that ferrets do not cough up their hairballs the way cats do — the hairball remedy helps the swallowed fur make its way through the ferret's digestive system. This can cause odd colored stools in ferrets with white fur.

Bathing your ferret when he is shedding is another way to help remove loose fur so your ferret doesn't swallow it.

Sabrina Says:™

DOUBLE-CHECK PRESCRIPTIONS

Any medication you give to your ferret is a serious matter, especially a prescription medication. If your veterinarian prescribes a particular medication for your ferret, make sure you understand exactly how to give it to the ferret. Ask your veterinarian to write down the dose and how often to give the medication. If something is not clear, ask. Giving your ferret the wrong dose can be very dangerous. Not giving the medication often enough or giving it too often can be dangerous too. Some medications, like antibiotics, are not effective if you give them for fewer days than what your veterinarian prescribed. Other medications, like prednisone, can be dangerous if you suddenly stop giving them.

Most of the time your veterinarian can dispense the medication he has prescribed for your ferret. Occasionally, however, he may not have the medication that your ferret needs and he will give you a written prescription to take to a pharmacist. If this occurs, make sure you know the name of the medication, whether a generic can be substituted, and the dosage for your ferret. Again, write it down so you know what the prescription is and what you should be getting from the pharmacist. When dropping off the prescription to be filled, *remind the pharmacist that the medication is for a ferret*, not for a person. Pharmacists are so used to dispensing medication for people that they might fill the prescription for your ferret thinking it is for a person; they may misread the dose because they expect it to be higher than what is actually written. If you have any questions about the dose or how often to give a medication to your ferret, ask your veterinarian.

We'd like to thank Margaret Merchant for her post on the internet Ferret Mailing List that reminded us of this.

See also "Don't Take Someone Else's Medicine" on page 30 and "Different Flavors!" on page 68.

My tips!

SAFE TOYS
(HIDDEN DANGERS OF CARDBOARD TUBES)

Safe toys are an important part of every ferret's play. Some toys may appear safe at first, but have hidden dangers. Empty paper tubes from toilet paper rolls are such a toy. Although they seem harmless, a busybody ferret could get one stuck on his head and not be able to remove it. This could give the ferret quite a panic. Many people cut a slit in the side of the tube to make it easier for a ferret to remove it while still allowing the ferret to play with it. Then again, some ferrets (like Marshmallow) like to chew on cardboard, making such toys totally inappropriate. It's up to you to decide what toys are safe and appropriate for your ferret and to monitor how your ferret plays with them.

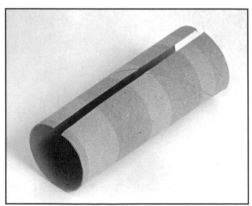

A slit in the side of a cardboard tube will help
prevent it from getting stuck on a ferret's head.

Marshmallow Explains It All™

LEND ME YOUR EARS

When I was a kit I used to get in trouble for sucking on Ralph's ears. At the time, the humans didn't understand what I was doing and figured I must be trying to annoy Ralph. Well, I wasn't. If I wanted to annoy Ralph I would have nipped at his neck or stolen his toys. I like Ralph; he's like my big brother. Though I do tease him from time to time, I like to do nice things for him. One of my favorite things to do for Ralph is help him to look sharp (you gotta look sharp!). I do this by helping him with his grooming.

See, when ferrets like each other — like I like Ralph — they groom each other. Part of that grooming is cleaning ears. (We also do that little nibbling thing on each other's fur, but that's another story.) Sometimes it looks like one of us is yanking on another one's ear or just sucking on the ear like a baby might do. But there is a purpose to all that licking and sucking; we're helping each other stay clean and healthy. We know you humans try to help out by scruffing us and cleaning our ears with some store-bought stuff. It is important that you help us out. But believe me, we like it much better when our friends clean our ears than when you humans do it. We use nice soft, warm, moist tongues to clean ears, while you humans use cotton swabs. (You call yourselves "civilized"!)

So the next time you pick up a ferret whose ears are all wet with ferret spit, you can be sure that he has a friend.

Sabrina Says:™

KEEP YOUR FERRET'S NAILS TRIMMED

Keeping your ferret well groomed keeps him healthy and happy. One of the important grooming tasks is nail clipping. If you don't keep your ferret's nails trimmed, they can split and get caught on blankets or on the ferret's cage. If this happens, the ferret can pull off his nail, which hurts. Sometimes the nail is so badly damaged that it doesn't grow back. Long nails can scratch people and other ferrets. Also, if a ferret has to walk around with really long nails, his toes will be forced to turn sideways, which can lead to permanent damage.

Trimming your ferret's nails is really easy. All you need is a nail clipper and something the ferret likes to lick (Ferretone, Ferretvite, Nutri-Cal). Put a few drops of Ferretone or a little dab of vitamin paste on the ferret's belly or on a clean surface (such as a spoon or a tongue depressor). While he's busy licking off it off, you can trim his nails with little or no fuss.

When clipping the nails, make sure you don't cut the quick (the red vein inside the nail). It's really easy to see since ferret nails are light colored and translucent. If you do cut the quick, you can put some styptic powder (available at a pet store) or flour on the bleeding tip of the nail, or you can dig the nail into a bar of white soap (Ivory). If you're not sure how short you can cut your ferret's nails, just trim off the longest part and do the nail trimming more often. Usually trimming your ferret's nails once a week is enough, but some ferrets need nail trimming more often, others less often.

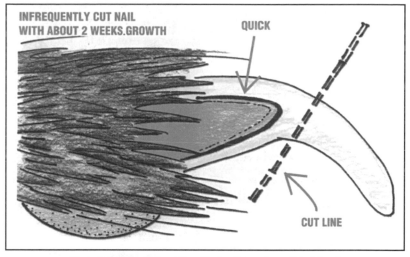

INFREQUENTLY CUT NAIL
WITH ABOUT 2 WEEKS.GROWTH

QUICK

CUT LINE

Illustration from *Modern Ferret* Issue #2 courtesy of Neal Segal

If you have two people, it is easiest for one person to hold the ferret (belly-side up, with a few drops of Ferretone on his belly) while the other trims the nails. When we trim nails, Eric holds the ferret and Mary does the clipping. Use one hand to hold the paw and separate the nail to be trimmed away from the others and the other hand to do the trimming. This helps in seeing the nail clearly, thus reducing the chances of cutting the nail too short or accidentally cutting a toe. The one holding the ferret makes sure the ferret doesn't squirm too much. If you don't have someone to help you trim nails, you can place the ferret on his back on your lap. Keep an eye on how quickly the ferret is licking the Ferretone off his belly so he doesn't finish licking before you finish clipping.

See also "Distracting Your Ferret With Lickable Treats" on page 136.

THE RADIATOR INCIDENT

In my never-ending quest for pesty activities, I have discovered yet another fun way to annoy my humans. I go inside the baseboard heaters. You might think you can't fit into these radiators, but if you're a ferret, you probably can.

First I rolled over on my back and used my paws to pull out the metal cover from the bottom. Then I stuck my nose in. Little by little, wriggle by wriggle, I managed to get just about half my body up into the radiator before my humans realized what I was doing. They pulled me out (try to explain "fun" to humans!).

That's when they went and blocked off all my access spots. Now I sometimes dig by the radiator until my humans come and pick me up. Being picked up is not as much fun as getting into the radiator, but it's not terrible. After all, what's life for if not getting all the attention?

Remember, stay pesty!

Temporarily Blocking the Radiator

We lived here for almost six months before Knuks noticed she could wriggle her way under and into the baseboard heating — a place we'd prefer not to have ferrets exploring. Since there's no distracting Knuks when she's on a Pest Mission, we had to remedy the situation before we could let the ferrets out the next day.

We devised a temporary way to block the bottom of the radiators. This will not work in the winter months, but for now it does. Eric and I wedged strips of wood (1 inch by 2 inches) under the radiator and placed a few bricks in front of the wood strips to prevent the stronger ferrets from pulling the wood out of place. Since we're renting the house and can't make any permanent changes, we like that the bricks and wood strips are removable.

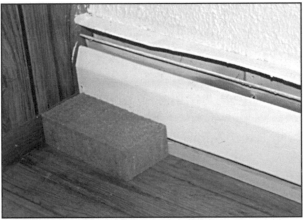

To keep the ferrets out of the radiators, we placed 1" by 2" strips of wood (in 6-foot lengths) under the radiators and placed bricks to prevent the ferrets from moving them. The bricks and wood were inexpensive and required no permanent changes to our rented house.

Making your house safe for ferrets — "ferret-proofing" — is an ongoing process. Ferrets are intelligent animals and tend to use their intelligence to discover new ways to cause mischief.

See also "Ferret-Proof" on page 82.

Trixie's Tips™

My tips!

PLAY IT SAFE!

It's a good idea to keep an extra close eye on your ferrets during any holiday season. Guests may not know how to be careful around ferrets or they may give ferrets treats they shouldn't have. The best thing to do is keep your ferrets in their cage when you have company over for the holidays. If your guests are staying overnight, make sure they know all the ferret rules so they don't do anything to endanger your ferrets. Make sure your guests know not to feed the ferrets anything you haven't said was OK. Guests don't mean to be clumsy, but sometimes they are without even realizing it. Make this season even better by preventing any ferret emergencies.

Here are some things to watch out for:
* Guests sitting or **stepping on ferrets**
* Guests feeding ferrets **foods they shouldn't have** (nuts, alcohol, sweets, dairy)
* Guests **letting ferrets outside** by mistake
* Children (or adults) **mishandling ferrets**
* **Decorations** your ferret might want to eat
* **Poisonous plants** (keep them well out of reach of ferrets)
* Ferrets getting into garbage bags (**check all trash** before taking it outside)
* Ferrets getting near active **fireplaces**, heat stoves, or candles

Also, if you're visiting relatives with your ferrets, keep in mind that your relatives haven't ferret-proofed their home. Make sure you create a safe spot for your ferrets to exercise and supervise them closely. If your relatives have pets, never leave them alone with your ferret.

Have lots of fun, but play it safe!

You should follow these tips any time you have visitors or parties. If you have children whose friends visit often, these tips should be used every day.

Marshmallow Explains It All ™

SHIVER ME TIMBERS!

Ferrets are warm-blooded creatures; our normal temperature is approximately 102°. But when we go to sleep, our temperature drops. That's one of the reasons we like to huddle together in a pile. When we wake up, we need to bring ourselves back up to normal. How do we do this? We shiver.

When I get out of hammock in the morning, I yawn and stretch a lot. I also do quite a bit of shivering. Shivering is how ferrets — and humans — warm themselves up. If, for example, you pick up your sleeping ferret and, in the process, wake him up, he will shiver. Some humans think this means the ferret is frightened. Nope. He's just chilly. If a ferret is frightened, he will usually stay very still (some less cultured ferrets might nip). The same is true for greeting your ferret as soon as you walk in the door after work or school. If your hands are cold and you pick up your warm ferret — whether he's asleep or awake — he will shiver. You might want to warm up those icy hands before you go picking up an unsuspecting toasty ferret. I know your ferret will thank you for it.

As for waking up sleeping ferrets, you might want to do it very gently. How many humans would tolerate being pulled out of a cozy bed? "Not I," you say. Now imagine if you were in a cozy bed all curled up with a bunch of warm fuzzy ferrets. See what I mean? Pick us up gently and keep us warm until we wake up.

Some of you more observant humans might notice that we ferrets sometimes shiver when we get a treat. For some of us this is just unbridled excitement. If we could eat the treat and do the happy dance (which I'll explain in a future column) at the same time, we would. Since we can't, we shiver. With other ferrets, if you pay close attention, you'll notice that they shiver when the human giving the treats is holding them with cold hands.

That's it until next time.

You'll want to keep a ferret's normal body temperature (102°F) in mind when setting the temperature for baths. What feels luke-warm to you feels cold to your ferret. Ferrets don't like cold baths and will struggle to get out if the water is too cold.

Sabrina Says:™

MAKE AN ISOLATION CAGE

If your ferret is sick or recovering from surgery, or if you think your ferret might be sick, you need to isolate that ferret from the other ferrets in your house. The best way to do this is to set up a special isolation cage. You can use a smallish one-level wire cage, a medium-sized dog carrier, or one of those small animal cages that has a plastic bottom and a removable coated wire top. If your ferret has had surgery or is weak and tends to lose his balance, the small animal cage or the dog carrier is probably better than the wire cage because they don't really have sharp edges the ferret might bump into.

The isolation cage should have all the things your ferret's regular cage has: a litter box, a water bottle and/or water dish, a food bowl, and a cozy, warm place to sleep.

If you think one of your ferrets is sick, separate him from the others so you can monitor him more closely. Count out the pieces of food you put in his food bowl so you can tell how many he eats — or if he's not eating at all. Check the ferret's food bowl often in case he eats all the food and needs more. Isolating a possibly sick ferret also lets you monitor his poop for anything out of the ordinary (diarrhea, foreign object, unusual color etc.). This way, if you have to take him to the veterinarian, you know the stool sample you bring with you is from the ferret who's sick.

If your ferret is recovering from surgery he needs time to regain his strength, and you need to be able to monitor his progress. As isolation cage makes it easy to monitor how much your ferret is eating, what his poop is like, and how he's acting. Also, if he has his own cage you don't have to worry about other ferrets, especially younger ones, trying to play with him or annoying him before he's well enough to handle it (young ferrets don't always know not to bother a sick ferret). Check with your veterinarian on how much playtime — if any — is OK for the sick or recovering ferret. Ferrets who have had surgery usually need a couple of days of rest so they don't pull out their stitches or overdo it. Sometimes we ferrets don't have the sense to sit still when we ought to.

Remember to thoroughly clean and disinfect the isolation cage (and everything in it, like hammocks, litter box, dishes, water bottle etc.) after a sick ferret is done using it so that it is clean and ready to go for the next time.

Marshmallow being housed in our travel carrier so we can monitor how much he is eating and pooping. He has his own food, water (bottle and drip cup), blankets, and his very own litter box.

My tips!

Trixie's Tips™

DIFFERENT FLAVORS!

Sometimes when your ferret is sick, your vet will want him to take prednisone to help him feel better. A lot of vets can give you liquid prednisone instead of pills. The liquid is flavored so that it doesn't taste bitter (prednisone is really bitter!). But if your ferret doesn't like how the flavoring tastes, it can be hard to get him to take it. A lot of medicines come in just one flavor, but liquid prednisone comes in different flavors. Hardly anyone here likes the grape flavor, but the cherry flavor is a big hit. So if your vet wants your ferret to take prednisone, ask if he has more than one flavor or if he can order another flavor. You can also get a prescription for PediaPred and get it at a pharmacy if your vet doesn't have a flavor of liquid prednisone that your ferret likes.

It's *really important* to check with your vet about the right dosage of prednisone to give your ferret. Different liquid prednisone brands could have different concentrations (we had one that was 1mg/1ml and another that was 1.34mg/1ml). Remember that you shouldn't stop giving prednisone suddenly. Talk to your vet about slowly cutting down the dosage when taking your ferret off prednisone.

Other medicines can often be flavored or given with a treat. Make sure you check with your vet before you mix a medicine with a treat to make sure it won't change the way the medicine works.

Why put more stress on a ferret who doesn't feel good? See if you can find medicine he doesn't hate.

Many medicines can be flavored so your ferret will take them more easily. If your veterinarian doesn't have a flavor your ferret will take, a compounding pharmacy may be able to help you. Make sure the pharmacist talks with your veterinarian about dosages, and remind the pharmacist that the medicine is dosed for a ferret not a human.

See also "Double-Check Prescriptions" on page 54.

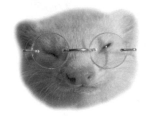

Marshmallow Explains It All™

HOW'S ABOUT A KIT?

I am a lifelong proponent of the philosophy: "The more the merrier." I joyously welcomed Knuks into the cage with open paws. When Trixie and Bosco arrived, I took the timid Bosco under my foreleg. Now Balthazar tugs at my ear, and I tolerate his exuberance with patience. Some call me "laid back." Others (rightly) call me "mellow."

However, there are things about which I become worked-up. For example, baby ferrets (properly termed "kits") require special care. In fact, all ferrets require special care, but kits in particular. Sometimes humans bring a kit into their home without first gathering the proper knowledge about the kit's care and — dare I use the word? — keeping.

As I have noted in previous columns, we ferrets are extraordinary beings. I am not being pompous or egotistical: at least one human, British writer Douglas Adams (*Hitchhiker's Guide to the Galaxy*) duly noted the undeniably integral role ferrets play in the universe. In his book *Life, the Universe, and Everything*, Mr. Adams clearly states that the answer to the question of life, the universe, and everything is 42, which is, of course, exactly the number of days required to create a ferret (also referred to as the gestation period). Coincidence? I think not.

Thus, ferrets being the center of all that exists, it surely follows that you humans who serve us ought to be darned honored to have the opportunity to serve us (by filling our food dishes and scooping our poop, et cetera).

Here, then, are some important guidelines for you to follow to help us maintain our vibrancy and *joie de vivre*.

First, not everyone who sells ferrets will give you correct information. As kits, we ferrets need a total of three vaccinations for distemper, the last one after 14 weeks of age (check with your veterinarian for your particular ferret's schedule — it should be based on the kit's age). In nearly all cases, the ferret breeder will have given the kit his or her first distemper shot. Rabies vaccinations can wait until the kit is at least 12 weeks old, though many humans wait until 14 weeks to give their ferrets this vaccination. It follows, then, that if you bring home an 8-week-old kit, he could not possibly have had "all" his shots. Yet, some humans feel compelled to tell those who are taking home a ferret kit that the kit is fully vaccinated. Not so! Do your own research. Obviously, you humans who have chosen to share your homes with a ferret are highly intelligent and have a wonderful ability to recognize the finer things in life. Your brilliance is evident in your choice of a ferret as a master ... I mean, pet. Of course, you exceptional humans are intellectually well equipped to do the right thing and learn about the needs of us ferrets.

Second, ferret kits do not have strong jaws. In many instances, they have only baby teeth. I had only just begun to grow in my adult teeth when my humans brought me to their home. As kits, we ferrets like it very much when our humans moisten our food so we can eat it more easily. Then, when we get a little older, we like to have a bit of a buffet: some moistened food and some crunchy food. When our adult teeth are fully grown in, we like to eat crunchy food.

Third, adult ferrets can sometimes be very rough with a new ferret kit. In most cases, the larger ferrets will not physically harm the kit. But the kit may be intimidated by the larger ferrets and become withdrawn. When I was but a kit, Ralph would throw me around mercilessly. Of course, now I'm bigger (and smarter) than he is and I can grab his scruff and throw him around. Though mostly we just curl up together and take long naps. The point is, however, that my humans had the presence of mind to keep a close eye on Ralph and me when I was still very small. This way they could intervene if I became too frightened or if Ralph really tried to hurt me. I handled Ralph fairly well, but Balthazar has had a terrible time trying to get along with him. Balthazar has even pooped on occasion because of Ralph's rough treatment. The two have come a long way, and we expect that soon they, too, will be curling up together.

Finally, remember that when you bring a kit into your home he tends to sleep very deeply, very often. But soon he reaches the age where he needs a good deal of exercise. By that I mean, a lot. A real lot. Give the tyke the time and space necessary for him to build his muscles and burn off his energy. He'll be sure to thank you for it; and torture you for it if you provide him insufficient opportunity to play.

I have but scratched the veneer of the important body of knowledge one must gain in order to properly care for a ferret in its smallest form — the kit. Above all, remember to love him and pay him the respect and adulation all ferrets deserve.

See also "Sleeping Like a Log" on page 15 and "Give a Kit a Smelly T-Shirt" on page 144.

CLIMBING MOUNT CAGEOUS

It's time for another lesson in how to create the most wonderful gift of all for your humans — mischief. Many humans believe that ferrets belong on the floor. They can be kinda silly like that. They don't realize that gravity simply doesn't apply to ferrets. Here's a way to get your humans riled up. It's fun and fulfilling!

First, keep a close eye on what your humans are doing. When they look away or get absorbed into the television, that's when you make your move. Nonchalantly walk over to the cage — be careful not to make it look like you're going to use the litter box (humans tend to take notice of such rare behaviors and tend to want to tell you how good you are). Timing is everything here, so don't get discouraged if you don't master this right away. Cage climbing is something that takes practice to get it just right. Just as the glaze settles on your human's eyes, make a fast break for it up the side of the cage. This should be easy since humans make cages from stuff that's just like ladders (you go figure why they then don't want you to climb them!).

Climbing the cage itself is pretty easy. Just put one paw over the other and up you go. Once you're at the top of the cage is when you should start trying to look very innocent and very confused. I'm not really sure what you're supposed to do once you're there but it sure is fun getting there.

When your human suddenly realizes that you're up in the air, it will usually get angry and shout a little. But don't worry about it. They don't mean it. When they come to take you off the top of the cage, you should cling to it as if your life depends on it. Once they get you off the cage, they'll usually give you lots of hugs and stuff like that — sometimes they waggle their finger at you. But you can just ignore all that.

After a few minutes you start all over again. Once you get good at this, you can keep your humans going all day and all night. It's good, clean fun!

Until next time — stay pesty!

When we first got ferrets, everything we read said that ferrets don't climb. They were all wrong. Although not all ferrets are climbers, the ones that are present a ferret-proofing challenge. Although they can climb fairly well when they put their minds to it, they are not nearly as good when it comes to getting back down. It's best to ferret-proof under the assumption that ferrets climb things.

Cage climbing presents a special challenge. If you have a big, tall cage like we do it can be a very real danger to ferrets who climb it. A fall from five feet (the height of our cage) can cause serious, life-threatening injury. There are two ways to prevent injury. You can keep your ferrets in a low cage so that a fall will be less likely to injure the ferret, or you can constantly supervise your ferret's play so you can prevent cage climbing (or rescue them once they have climbed up).

Sabrina Says:™

PREVENTING ESCAPES

Losing a ferret is a very difficult thing, especially when it could have been prevented. Now that the weather is warm and you are opening windows and doors, it is particularly important to keep a close eye on your ferrets. A lot of ferrets get out of their houses because someone didn't latch the screen door or because the window screen was loose or had a hole in it.

If your ferrets will have access to a window, try to keep that window closed (and locked). If you can't, then make sure the screen is secure — and check it often in case a ferret scratches at it (he could make his own escape hole!). If your ferrets are allowed access to rooms with a door to the outside (e.g., living room, kitchen, den), now is the time to take extra safeguards to prevent an escape. Fix any screen doors that don't close or latch properly.

Air conditioners can also create a problem for your ferrets. Make sure your A/C units are fitted properly and securely into windows. Take the time to firmly block any area around the unit that a ferret might be able to slip through (if a ferret can get his head through, he can get his body through, too). Window fans should also be fitted properly into windows to prevent a ferret from getting out (or getting injured!).

Make sure everyone in your household is aware of the ferrets in your home, even — and especially — house-guests. If you have children who come in and go out all day, consider keeping the ferrets in their cage until evening when the children are in for the day.

Remember that ferrets cannot live on their own outside. Most ferrets only make it a few days before they die from exposure, are hit by a car, or are injured by a dog they thought might be friendly. Even people who don't know what a ferret is might harm your pet if he gets outside. So take some time and make your home as escape-proof as possible.

Have a great and safe summer!

This column ran in a spring issue of *Modern Ferret*, but the advice is relevant throughout the year, especially in warmer climates.

Dear Gabby

YOUR ADVICE FERRET

BOYS AND GIRLS GET ALONG

Dear Gabby:

My mommy wants to get me a brother, but she's worried that boys and girls can't get along. What should she do?

— Brotherless in Seattle

Dear Brotherless:

Since your mommy is just keeping you as pets, you are probably spayed and your new brother will probably be neutered. It's better and healthier for ferrets to be that way if they are not being bred. Altered boy and girl ferrets can all get along. It is important to remember that ferrets are individuals and, just like people, not every two will like each other. It will help if your mom takes you along to choose your new brother — you might even check a local club or shelter to see if there are any nice boys who need a home.

Although most neutered ferrets get along fine, especially when the new ferret introduced is a kit, sometimes it takes a little work, patience, and time to integrate a new ferret. Because ferrets are individuals, you may encounter personality conflicts from time to time. To help the ferrets get used to each other during the integration process, try switching the sleeping blankets between the two ferrets so each gets used to the other's unique smell.

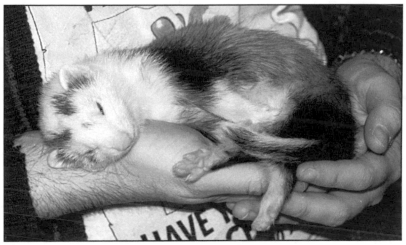

Gabby's Tip of the Day:
A nap in the hand is worth two in the hammock.

Marshmallow Explains It All™

BOTTLE-BRUSH TAIL

Things can sometimes get a bit out of paw when ferrets wrestle with each other. When that happens, the tail of one or the other brawler might stand on-end much like a bottle-brush. This physiological phenomenon is referred to as "bottle-brush tail." It may also be referred to as "puffy" or "poofy" tail, or the more descriptive "bristle" tail. Sometimes it is used as a verb ("Knuks bottle-brushes when Bosco sits on her").

Whatever one calls it, it does occur in all ferrets from time to time. Some ferrets bottle-brush more than others; some cause bottle-brushing more than they experience it themselves. Most humans tend to take bottle-brushing as a sign that things are getting a bit too rough in the play between ferrets and they break up the tussle. While bottle-brushing is often no more than an involuntary response to a stressful situation (the other ferret is winning in a routine hierarchy struggle), it also occurs when there is a serious problem between two ferrets. Humans should use good judgment when any ferret bottle-brushes. I recommend giving the ferrets a short break to regain their composure (or plan a better strategy).

Ferrets can also get bottle-brush tails when they are very excited about investigating a new environment. This occurs particularly in new environments that have an abundance of new and interesting smells. Knuks demonstrates excitement-induced bottle-brush tail in the photo. In these cases, humans tend to point and giggle, apparently unconcerned about the fact that fascinating aroma discoveries are being made right under their obviously inferior proboscises.

Many humans believe they do not have any experiences in common with their ferrets' bottle-brush tails. I beg to differ (I also beg for treats, but that's another column). I have seen episodes of *The Munsters* where the scared people get bottle-brush head. Now *that's* ridiculous. But I always knew humans were a bit backward.

So the next time your ferret's tail gets all puffy, make sure you assess the situation and take action as necessary. But please, no jokes about scrubbing the water bottles.

Knuks demonstrates bottle-brush tail
while exploring a new room.

Sabrina Says:™

FERRET-PROOF!

Ferret-proofing your home can save your ferret's life. Some people don't realize that they have to make their homes safe for their new fuzzy friends. But ferrets are pure curiosity, so they need to be supervised and their environment needs to be made safe. Of course, you can never make your home "proof" against ferret curiosity, but you can create a place where your ferret is unlikely to get hurt. And if you keep an eye on your ferrets, you will be able to remove any new dangers that they might find.

Ferrets can get into just about anything — or out of anything. Before you let a ferret run around in your house, you need to make sure there are no ways for the ferret to get outside. (Ferrets can only survive a couple of days outside on their own.) You will have to seal up any holes in the walls, repair any doors that don't close well, and secure windows that the ferret can push open.

You also need to make sure your furniture is safe for your ferret. That means moving reclining chairs and foldout beds out of the area your ferret will be playing in. Many ferrets get crushed in the mechanism of "moving" furniture. Don't let this happen to your ferret.

Appliances can be a hazard to ferrets. Stoves, dishwashers, and refrigerators all have moving or hot parts underneath them. Dryers can be very inviting to a ferret in search of a place to nap. The best thing to do is make kitchens and laundry rooms off-limits to your ferrets. If you can't do that, take precautions so your ferret doesn't get hurt. Always check laundry baskets before doing laundry. Check the dishwasher before you run it. Make sure no ferrets are sleeping under or behind kitchen appliances before you turn them on.

Check ferret toys regularly for signs of wear that could make them unsafe.

If there is some unusual activity going on such as furniture moving, appliance or plumbing repairs, guests who don't know about ferrets, etc. — the safest place for your ferrets to be is in their cage. You can let them out again after things have returned to normal.

With some thought and a bit of effort, you can keep your ferret happy and safe in your home. Remember that not everything a ferret wants to do is safe for a ferret to do.

Ferret intelligence is geared towards problem solving. This can present challenges for ferret owners because the problems ferrets try to solve often lead to mischief (e.g., "How can I knock over that glass of soda?" "Where should I hide this glove?" "What is inside this wallet?").

By regularly providing your ferret with new sources of intellectual stimulation, you will help him have more fun and expend his intellectual energy in appropriate ways. Try to rotate toys (remove toys when your ferret grows bored with them and bring them back a few weeks later so they seem "new" again). Also, give your ferret some challenges such as learning tricks (begging or rolling over for a treat) or finding hidden treats.

My tips!

Trixie's Tips™

CHEAP TOYS!

Ferret toys don't have to cost a lot. Sometimes clever parents can find that the least expensive things will make us the happiest.

We found these nifty hard plastic balls in the machines you see after you check out at the supermarket. These balls were only 25¢ each (so you can get a bunch!). The hard plastic is very durable and even the big boys have a hard time trying to hurt them (some of the big boys here like to break ping pong balls).

Some ferrets just like to stash them, some like to play "nose soccer" with them, and some ignore them (good thing they're cheap!).

The balls come with all different designs on them. Knuks likes the soccer ball — I think she likes to watch the black-and-white pattern as she noses the ball all around the room. Some ferrets prefer the larger smiley face ball (it cost 50¢). Big boy ferrets can carry the smaller balls around in their mouths! Some ferrets like the fake eyeball — yuck!

As with all toys, watch for wear or breakage and take it away if it breaks (replace it with something else).

Ferrets are a lot like young children, preferring to play with the box a new toy came in over the toy itself. Many of the things ferrets enjoy can be inexpensive. Items like empty boxes, clean plastic soda bottles, old socks, and clean film canisters are favorites at our house. You can also make a dangling toy by tying a toy onto a stick with a piece of string. When she was younger, Sabrina loved chasing a crumpled piece of paper dangled from a string. Provide new toys or rotate toys regularly to keep your ferret intellectually stimulated and happy.

Examine every toy regularly for signs of wear or breakage. Since every ferret plays differently, what may be an appropriate, safe toy for one ferret may be a dangerous toy for another.

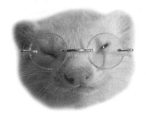

Marshmallow Explains It All™

MARSHMALLOW'S GUIDE TO FINE DINING IN YOUR OWN LIVING ROOM

When humans hide food in various remote corners of their homes it is often considered a sign of a fixation and is usually looked upon with a raised eyebrow. But ferrets are not to be judged by such standards. A stronger force compels our desire for out-of-cage dining: Instinct. We do not remove crunchies from our food bowls and place them in special spots through-out our domestic domain because we are messy. Nor do we do it simply to hear our humans shriek about "wasted food" on vacuuming day (which is, by the way, something akin to Arma-geddon for some of us ferrets with sensitive tympanic mem-branes and soft courage — shudder). No. Simply: We stash food because we must.

Our ancestor and closest relative is the Polecat (European or Steppe — take your pick). Although these wild animals' be-haviors differ from ours in many ways, some of those behaviors remain with us ferrets — even though they make little sense in our domestic environments. And even though we do not know why we perform these behaviors. How many of you humans have asked your ferrets: "Why must you hide these crunchies behind the television stand when you have a whole bowlful in your cage? Have I ever denied you copious crunchies? Then, Heavens, why must you act as if crunchies are going out of style?" Sound familiar?

Most ferrets cannot answer your questions because they do not know why they hide their food (also because most have taken a vow of silence with respect to humans — but that is another story). Being a ferret of advanced intelligence, I do know why we hide our food and I can give you the answers you seek.

Polecats are solitary animals that live within a set area or range, which they consider to be their "turf" (to use a word with which you humans are familiar). This area can be quite considerable in size when compared with the size of the average human home. Within his range the polecat has several domiciles, much like ostentatious humans have a house in the country, a studio apartment in the city, and a villa in the south of France. This way if there is danger or if they become tired or injured, they are never very far from home even though their "turf" is a large area. Of course, the polecat must stock the larders — so to speak — of all his various homes. Those humans who have enormous freezers in their basements chock-full of frozen pizzas and little cocktail franks in pastry will understand the need to hoard food for any potentiality. The polecat, then, is much like a Boy Scout and says through his actions what the Scouts say through the slogan: "Be prepared."

This stashing behavior is one that was not entirely bred out of us ferrets during our many centuries of domestication. Thus, we take the crunchies from the copiously stocked bowl and place them strategically throughout our "range" — even if that range is only a single room. We must be prepared for the moment we feel the vague rumblings of hunger while we are playing behind the television cart — after all, the cage is several steps from the television. Besides, food eaten outside the cage has a certain je ne sais quoi about it. There's allure to crunchies munched behind the couch.

The bottom line is this: do not try to reason with your ferret when he trots off, mouth overstuffed with kibble, to some remote corner of his play area. You will not train this behavior out of him. But do make sure to clean up the morsels every so often so you don't get bugs and so your ferret doesn't become ill from eating very old food.

Bon Appétit!

A popular game at our house consists of sitting on the floor and handing out pieces of the ferrets' regular crunchy food one by one. The ferrets all run up to grab a piece of food and run off with it. Some even stand on their hind legs and beg. Since we are giving them the same nutritious food they usually eat, there is no danger of "over-treating" them. They just appreciate the special way in which the food is given.

Sabrina Says:™

BITING ELECTRICAL CORDS

Sometimes we ferrets are not as smart as we wish we were. Like many ferrets, Trixie likes to bite on electrical cords. This is very dangerous, but she can't understand that. To prevent any tragedies, try putting a few dabs of Bitter Apple paste on exposed electrical cords. Once a ferret notices that all electrical cords have a terrible taste, she will begin to avoid them. Make sure your ferrets have plenty of appropriate toys they can chew on. Gumabones (by the same company that makes Nylabones) are tough enough to withstand a ferret's strong jaws and sharp teeth, without being hard. Whenever your ferret tries to bite on electrical cords, offer her a Gumabone instead. Trixie's learning!

P.S. Always monitor the toys you give your ferrets. So far, nobody here has managed to harm a Gumabone (in several years of use) — but you can never be sure! That's just the way we ferrets are!

Offering your ferret an appropriate chew toy can help you train him out of chewing on dangerous things like electrical cords. Hyper-Fur makes a product, called a Cheweasel, that is an edible chew toy for ferrets. For more information contact Hyper-Fur Ferrets' Products, 6820 Santa Monica Blvd. #123, Los Angeles, CA 90038.

My tips!

THINK PINK!

Here's a great book you can recommend to your vet. It is the most up-to-date reference on ferret medicine currently available. If your veterinarian doesn't have it, you might think of giving him or her a copy as a present this holiday season.

Ferrets, Rabbits, and Rodents: Clinical Medicine and Surgery. Edited by Elizabeth V. Hillyer, DVM, and Katherine E. Quesenberry, DVM. Published in 1997 by W.B. Saunders Company, Philadelphia. ISBN 0-7216-4023-0.

To order direct from the publisher
(US, Canada & Mexico), call toll free:
   1-800-545-2522
Or write:
   WB Saunders Company, Orlando
   6277 Sea Harbor Dr
   Orlando FL 32887-4800
All other countries:
   Tel 44 181 300 3322
   Harcourt Brace and Company
   Footscray High St
   Sidcup, Kent
   DA14 5HP
   UK
Or visit the website at http://www.hbuk.co.uk/wbs

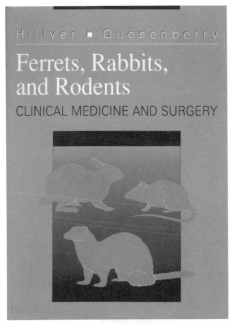

Ferrets, Rabbits, and Rodents is often called the "Pink Book" due to its pink (magenta) cover

Other useful resource books:

Essentials of Ferrets: A Guide for Practitioners. By Karen Purcell, DVM. Published in 1999 by AAHA Press. ISBN 0-9414-5173-9.

Biology and Diseases of the Ferret. Second Edition. Edited by James G. Fox, DVM. Published in 1998 by Lippincott, Williams & Wilkins. ISBN 0-6833-0034-2.

Ferrets: Health, Husbandry and Diseases. By Maggie Lloyd, MA, Vet MB, Cert LAS, MRCVS. Published in 1999 by Blackwell Science Ltd (UK). ISBN 0-6320-5178-7.

You can order any of these books through the FerretWare catalog at 1-800-FERRETWare. Proceeds from FerretWare sales benefit California Domestic Ferret Association (CDFA) rescue and educational programs. www.ferretware.com

Marshmallow Explains It All™

THE FALL FASHIONS

The usual autumn ferret fashion trends are back — rounder bellies, thicker fur, and the occasional dramatic coat color change. What we're seeing on the *ferret walk* is a lot of full, round lines. The well-dressed ferret wouldn't be caught out about town without a plush undercoat this winter.

Every fall, ferrets prepare themselves for the colder months by growing in a thick undercoat and adding a bit of "padding" (that is, fat). This change is initiated by the shortening length of daylight, not by a drop in temperature.

Also in vogue for the winter months are subtle shading highlights. Although albinos like myself rarely, if ever, indulge in even the most modest novelty, colored ferrets may yield to the playful trends in color variety — many opting for a lighter shade of their natural color. Certainly the hottest mask-shape trend is moving from broad face coverage to just a hint of a shadow on the bridge of the nose and brow. Panda ferrets are often on the cutting edge with bold color alterations; facial markings, if any, are understated this season for the trend-setting Panda or Blaze.

For ferrets "of a certain age," the natural look is definitely *in*. As some ferrets reach their golden years, they experience a fashion phenomenon referred to as *roaning*. As white hairs replace colored guard hairs, the *roaned* ferret takes on an angelic white-silver glow. Roaning is similar to the human phenomenon of "going gray"; among fashion-forward mustelids it is considered *trés chic*.

During these fall fashion changes, we ferrets require a certain amount of special pampering so we can look and feel our best. As we are shedding our old coats, it is important that you, our human attendants, make efforts to ensure we do not get an intestinal blockage (or partial blockage) because we are swallowing hair when we groom ourselves. Offer a hairball remedy (usually labeled for cats and most commonly flavored with malt) every other day (or every day if we are coughing as a result of the hair). Give about a half-inch- to an inch-long ribbon depending on the size of your ferret.

Humans can also help facilitate ferret make-overs by brushing your ferret to remove loose fur. Bathing — no more than once every two weeks — can help remove loose fur, too. What fashion-conscious ferret wouldn't appreciate an impeccably arranged boudoir? Humans can help by frequently changing fur-covered blankets and hammocks to keep the ferret's décor sparkling.

Finally, some ferrets will enjoy helping others with their new wardrobe, so if you have a ferret that is grooming other ferrets (but may not be going through his own coat change), he might need some hairball remedy too.

That's it from the world of ferret fashion until spring, when we can look forward to the return of sleeker lines and slimmer waistlines.

Sabrina Says:™

LAPPING WATER FROM A DISH IS FUN!

Not all ferrets understand the principle of lapping water from a dish. Some stick their paws into the water and try to scoop it out — much to the dismay of nearby ferrets who would have preferred to remain dry. Others attempt to scuba dive in the water dish; lifting out their soaking wet heads to shake off the water and spray those same nearby dry ferrets. Never mind that these uncivilized ferrets get water all over the blankets and any food dishes that are too close to the water dish — not to mention the floor outside the cage. Forget about those ferret owners who make the mistake of placing the water dish too close to the litter box (talk about a mess!).

There is a solution — a way to help these ferrets learn the proper, acceptable way to lap water from a dish.

Start with only a small amount of water — this will discourage the scuba divers, though the paw splashers may not be deterred (they might even be encouraged).

Next, put a *few drops* of oil-based coat supplement (e.g., Ferretone or Furotone) on top of the water. It is important to only put a few drops in the water. Ferrets understand that they should lick the Ferretone and by default they lap the water. A few sessions of this should help your ferrets learn what the dish of water is for. Even the paw splashers should get the idea.

Of course, some ferrets will never learn. For those there are water bottles, thank goodness.

Remember that if you use this method to teach your ferrets to lap their water, you will need to wash the water dish daily so no oils build up on the surface. This teaching method should be used only short-term; if you have ferrets who just won't learn, give them a water bottle instead.

Happy lapping!

It is also a good idea to provide lapping water in a dish that attaches to the cage. Several types of attachable dishes (for food or water) are available at pet stores.

Even if you have ferrets that are good with lapping water, you should still provide them with a water bottle to make sure they don't accidentally run out of water.

Marshmallow Explains It All™

AIN'T MISBEHAVIN'

There are tomes dedicated to the so-called normal behaviors of ferrets, but no scholarly treatise can hold a candle to good, old-fashioned astute observation when it comes to knowledge about an individual ferret. For whatever might be a normal behavior for all ferrets, there are also behaviors that are normal for a particular ferret. Case in point: Koosh, for some reason of which only he is aware, is compelled to dig in the water dish as if it were filled with soil. While a dignified ferret such as myself would never stoop to such barroom antics, it is a normal behavior for the likes of him. However, this type of behavior is but a fraction of the amalgam of behaviors that make up the ferret's normal repertoire. There are also eating and drinking behaviors, litter-box behaviors, play behaviors, and social behaviors, to list but a few.

Because a ferret's agenda is much more pressing than that of any human, the responsibility for detecting changes in normal ferret behavior patterns rests solely and squarely upon the shoulders of the fur-deficient, two-legged treat-dispenser.

To be able to recognize when a ferret is behaving in a manner out of the ordinary, one must first establish what constitutes "the ordinary." There is but one way to accomplish this objective: observe your ferrets' routines. Since humans seem to be enamored of examples, I offer this one: The always lovely

Sabrina is world renowned for her impeccable litter-box deportment. Should one of our humans upon a day discover this dear ferretess defecating in an unsuitable area, that human should not fail to take note. For a scoundrel such as Bosco da Gama the random placement of feces outside the litter box is common practice, much to the dismay of his more refined brethren. However, for a lady such as Sabrina this lack of consideration for others is contrary to expectation. Thus, depending upon the circumstances of the incident, the human should consider whether Sabrina requires medical attention.

To be sure, divergence from routine does not always call for concern. Humans need to employ good judgment in determining whether a change in behavior is a potential sign of illness or a simple attempt to break free of the "ferret race," if you will. Key to this determination is the knowledge gained by the keen observation of the exquisite minutiae of everyday ferret existence. In other, simpler terms: knowing your ferrets will help you recognize when something is wrong.

Enjoy the show.

Ferrets are small and they have a fast metabolism, so illness usually appears quickly. Being observant means you can recognize illness and get the ferret medical attention quickly. For many illnesses, early detection and treatment can mean the difference between life and death.

Sabrina Says:™

USE A PET CARRIER TO TRANSPORT YOUR FERRET

One of the best investments you can make as a ferret owner (besides the ferret, of course) is a pet carrier for trips to the veterinarian or to visit friends. Pet carriers come in various shapes, sizes, and colors, and you can find one to fit your budget.

Don't allow your ferret to roam free in your car, it can be dangerous. He can get caught under a pedal or he can dig around and get into somewhere dangerous (like the engine). He could also get out an open window, even if it's only partly open. He can get caught in the door if you get out of the car. If you are in a car accident and your ferret is loose in the car, he could get thrown around and hurt. Or if he isn't hurt that way, he could escape from the car. Your ferret has a much better chance of surviving if he is in a carrier. Also, a rescue worker might not want to pick up a loose ferret to remove it from a wrecked car, but very few people, if any, would have a problem taking out a pet carrier.

It is by far safer to keep your ferret in a carrier when he is traveling. Most ferrets don't mind too much as long as it is not a very long trip. For longer trips, you'll want to get a larger carrier and make some stops along the way so your ferret can get some exercise (on a harness and leash if you're walking at a rest stop).

Many states have laws that require people to wear seat belts and keep their small children in proper car seats. Think of a pet carrier as the proper car seat for your ferret.

If you are traveling long distance (especially crossing state lines) make sure you have hand-signed (not stamped) proofs of vaccination from your veterinarian.

To help make the trip easier on your ferrets, bring plenty of water from home (the water they are used to drinking) to prevent any possibility of digestive upset. Also bring enough food from home — not all brands are available everywhere.

REARRANGING THE LITTER BOX

Hey kids! There's a really great way to get your humans' attention and you can do it even when you're locked in your cage (which makes this a particularly pesty project!).

Forget about digging in the litter box. That's for amateurs. If you've got the true pesty spirit you know that moving the litter box to where *you* want it can drive your humans nuts.

It's always best to be prepared to put your whole body into your work. First, stick your nose behind the litter box and then wriggle your front paws in there too. Now you're in position to start shoving the litter box away from the side of the cage. This works great for litter boxes outside the cage too. If you're a petite pest, like me, you might need to use both your front and back legs to move heavy litter boxes.

For the more advanced pest, there's a slightly harder, but much more rewarding, variation on the moving the litter box trick. It's called *dumping the litter box*. Any pest worth her Ferretone knows that dumping the litter box is way better than just throwing the litter around. The most challenging part of this project is getting either your nose or your paw under the litter box. It is best to lie on your back to do this. Some ferrets aren't really coordinated, so this might take practice. Once you've got your front paws under the litter box, heave it up over your back paws too. You will be holding up the litter box on your four paws. Now kick! You probably won't manage to dump the whole box at once, especially if you're a beginner. But keep trying. Eventually you'll be able to dump the litter box completely upside-down. Talk about an attention-getter!

Of course, my litter-dumping days are over since my humans figured out how to anchor the litter box to the cage. Now I have to just dig in the litter box and hope that I can toss enough litter out with my tiny paws to get my humans' attention. I'm counting on you kids to carry on the pesty crusade.

Now get to it! There are litter boxes to be tossed around. And always, stay pesty!

— Knuks

Locked in place! How frustrating!

Discovering "C" Clamps

Ferrets like to rearrange their environment, especially their litter boxes. Although your ferret might enjoy rearranging the litter boxes, it can be a messy problem for you. Not only do you end up with litter all over the place, but because the litter box isn't where it belongs, someone furry will invariably use the area where the litter box used to be as if the litter box were still there.

We came up with a solution to the litter-box moving and dumping problems — "C" clamps. They are inexpensive and you can get them at any hardware store. We use the 1-inch size "C" clamps to hold our ferrets' litter boxes in place in their cage. They hold the litter boxes in place securely and they are relatively easy to remove when it's time to clean the boxes. "C" clamps prevent ferrets from moving the litter box aside and they prevent anyone furry from getting underneath the litter box and dumping its contents.

Now we have a much neater cage for our ferrets, which makes everyone happy. Except Knuks, who is sort of disappointed that we spoiled her fun.

Trixie's Tips™

My tips!

WALK LIKE ME!

Ferrets, and especially ferret kits, often like to be really underfoot. Unlike most cats and dogs, ferrets never seem to learn to watch out for where you are stepping. For new ferret owners, this can take a lot of getting used to. Many ferret owners opt to walk with a "shuffle step" — sliding their feet across the floor instead of taking normal steps. This way they avoid accidentally stepping on tiny ferret feet. Remember that when non-ferret owners come to visit (as often happens around the holidays) that it is your responsibility to show them how to be careful around your ferrets — so teach them the "shuffle step!"

Marshmallow Explains It All™

THE TRICK OF THE TREAT

My editor has informed me that this issue's theme is Halloween. I enjoy so-called holidays as much as the next journalist, so I have decided to write this column in the spirit (intentional pun) of Halloween.

What is Halloween? To me, it is an unsatisfactory excuse for miniature humans to collect and carry with them as many treats as their nubby little paws can hold. But why would one require any excuse for unabashed treat-collecting? Is it not a noble goal? Indeed, does not the ferret seek to attain this goal every day of his life? However, we ferrets are thwarted at every turn in our quest for more treats. Why? The consuming of treats is one of the rare instances where the ordinarily unenlightened human knows better than the ordinarily ingenious ferret. Of course, I am the exception to that rule, as I am a ferret of the highest caliber. Thus, it falls upon my shoulders to educate those among you humans who are wanting in *treat-smarts*.

Ferrets are carnivores. As such, we are not well equipped to digest fruits and vegetables. But we love treats; and our humans love to give us treats (as it should be). The best treats are the ones that are good for us (e.g., pieces of cooked meat or hard-boiled egg — foods a carnivore can sink his teeth into). But the vast majority of us want more than just a trifling piece of meat. It is up to you humans to make sure we ferrets get only a minimum amount of non-meat treats. Many of us like various fruits and vegetables (e.g., bananas, green beans), but these should be offered only in moderation; some foods (e.g., nuts, alcohol) should not be offered at all. Sweet treats (e.g., candy, soda) are not good for us, though most of us would sell our grandmothers for them. Humans should never offer so many treats to a ferret that he will not eat his regular food. If your ferret has an illness like insulinoma (as I have), you need to be especially careful not to offer a treat that might cause a dramatic change in his insulin level. For us, high-protein treats (like meat) are a good choice. Check with your veterinarian.

If your ferret is too sophisticated to get caught up in the treat hoopla (which is considered the mark of a superior mustelid in some circles), you can offer him a piece or two of his regular food from your hand. He'll like that.

Some ferrets will learn how to do tricks for their treats. Which makes me wonder why so few miniature humans do tricks anymore — instead they just demand a treat. They could learn something from us ferrets. Actually, they could learn an abundance of things from us ferrets — like persistence, a constant desire to learn and explore new opportunities, and the benefits of getting enough sleep. Speaking of sleep, I believe it's my naptime. Until next time...

See also "Hold the Veggies, Please" on page 28.

Sabrina Says:™

BE NICE TO FERRETS
WHO CAN'T SEE YOU

Ferrets can go blind as a result of several different things. Though I don't have cataracts like our friend Pumba in the accompanying photo, I did lose my sight a few months ago. For the most part, ferrets adapt pretty well to blindness. Many humans are surprised at how well a blind ferret can get along. But ferrets have a great sense of smell, which helps them to get around and find things like the food dish and the litter box, even when they can't see those things.

When I first lost my sight, I didn't want to run around very much because I'd bump into the furniture. Playing with other ferrets was frustrating because they could move really fast and I'd miss them when I tried to jump on them. But now I can run across the room and I can even home-in on whistles so I know where to go to get a treat. Most of the time I don't run into anything as long as the humans don't move the furniture or put new things in my way. See, I sort of memorized where everything in the living room is. The humans try to help me by talking to me and letting me sniff them before they pick me up so I don't get startled. They also try to point out when they have to put something new in the room so I don't get surprised by it. I wish the other ferrets were that nice to me!

If you think your ferret is going blind or has gone blind, take him to your veterinarian. There may be something your vet can do to help. At least he can confirm that your ferret can no longer see. Just make sure you're extra nice to any ferrets who can't see you anymore. They'll like that.

Photo of Pumba, owned by Nina Trischitta and John Freer of Lindenhurst, New York. Pumba has cataracts in both eyes and is completely blind.

Sabrina later developed cataracts, although she was blind already.

My tips!

FERRET BRUSHES!

It's a good idea to brush your ferret if she's shedding. Brushing helps to get the loose fur off the ferret. If you don't brush out the loose fur, your ferret can swallow it while she's cleaning herself. When your ferret swallows a lot of fur, it can get bunched together after a while and cause a blockage or a partial blockage in your ferret's stomach. Sometimes your vet will have to perform an operation to get the blockage out of your ferret. So it's really much better to just use a brush to get the fur *off* the ferret before the fur gets *in* the ferret.

There are a few different kinds of brushes you can find at your local pet supply store. There's what's called a "slicker" brush, which is sort of like a rake. Then there's a brush with soft bristles like cats use. My humans also found a brush that's made for cats that has rubber spikes (it's the thing on the right in the picture). All of these brushes work for brushing your ferret. Different ferrets like the way different brushes feel, so you might want to try a couple different styles of brush on your ferret. Some ferrets don't really like being brushed, but if you keep at it in short sessions, your ferret can get used to it — and even get to like it.

It's best to give a treat after a brushing. Just because.

Note:

Many ferret owners also give their ferrets a hairball remedy to help them pass any hair that they do swallow. There are several brands of hairball remedy for ferrets now available at pet stores. A bath can also help remove loose hair from your ferret.

L to R — slicker wire brush, pet brush, Zoom Groom (Kong)

Marshmallow Explains It All ™

TAKING YOUR LUMPS... OFF

I am a philosophical ferret. I cast aside my emotions in favor of pure logic when I am faced with a decision. I do not fear the veterinarian; he is my friend. So the thought of having an unusual growth removed from my body was not daunting. It seemed like the only logical course of action.

While I was playing with the youngsters one evening, my humans noticed what appeared to be a scab on my shoulder. I tried to tell them that it was not the result of a tussle with the beastly young Balthazar, but something more. All in vain. My humans chose to wait a couple of days before conveying me to the veterinarian. I do wish they could learn to speak Ferret-ese.

The veterinarian agreed with my humans that a period of observation was appropriate, considering that I had been engaged in rough play with the youngsters. The scab healed, though there remained a slight bump. Then the scab reappeared a few days later. My humans took me back to the veterinarian, and all concurred that the growth should be removed. The veterinarian removed the bump while I was under a local anesthetic (I found that the vet could speak a smattering of Ferret-ese and understood my desire to observe the simple procedure).

A biopsy was performed on the removed tissue. The laboratory reported that the growth was a mast cell tumor — benign. Mast cell tumors of the skin are fairly common in ferrets. They are almost always benign growths. It is important to remove these tumors as they will spread if not removed. In addition, they are very itchy. It is because my mast cell tumor was itchy that the humans discovered it when they did — I had scratched at it until a scab formed.

The day after the veterinarian removed the stitches from the first procedure, my humans noticed a bump on my forehead. This time they did not hesitate, but brought me back to the veterinarian immediately to have the bump removed. For this procedure, the veterinarian administered general anesthesia. It was just as well, since I could not see the bump and would not have been able to observe the procedure. As of this writing, I have had no further bumps.

Since most ferrets are not as logical-minded as I am, it is important for humans to take the initiative and periodically check their ferrets' bodies for lumps and bumps. Any bump should be brought to the attention of the ferret's veterinarian. It is usually best to have the growth removed and biopsied — regardless of the ferret's protestations. Your ferret will thank you when the growth has been removed and the itchiness subsides.

Concerns about the use of general anesthesia in ferrets have been greatly reduced by the routine use of isoflurane gas. Ferrets wake up more quickly from isoflurane anesthesia than from other forms of anesthesia.

Ferrets have a rapid metabolism and do not require the longer fasting times before surgery that other animals usually require. In general, fasting times are often between 4 and 6 hours prior to surgery. Shorter fasting times are recommended in ferrets that might have insulinoma. Discuss with your veterinarian what is an appropriate fasting time for your ferret.

Sabrina Says:™

FIND OUT WHAT HAPPENED (POST-MORTEM EXAMINATIONS)

This is a somewhat delicate subject for some people, but it may be a very important one. Sukie Crandall, one of our friends from Basking Ridge, New Jersey, made this suggestion and I think it's good.

Losing a ferret is a very sad event for the humans and the other ferrets in the home. The sadness is compounded by shock when a ferret dies for no apparent reason. Even though this is a difficult time, it is important to have your veterinarian determine what caused the ferret's death. In some cases, it might be an internal problem that showed no symptoms. (Marshmallow showed no symptoms despite having an adrenal growth that would have eventually caused his death — thankfully it was discovered before then.)

One reason for doing a post-mortem examination (autopsy) is to find out if the ferret died from some kind of poison — whether it was a household chemical or some other substance. This is important because you would want to be able to remove the problem before it affects other ferrets or other animals or children in your home. Also, if the ferret died of something that is contagious to other ferrets (or to people) you would want to know so you could seek medical attention for the other ferrets. Sometimes it just helps to know what happened so you don't wonder about whether you could have prevented it. This can help you with the grief over losing your ferret.

Of course, an autopsy isn't always possible. Sometimes it can be too much of an expense. But you should consider it in the case of a sudden or unexplained death.

It has become more socially acceptable to recognize that our pets have a special place in our lives and that the death of a pet is a great loss that requires time to grieve. Although there are still people who do not understand how painful the death of a pet can be, many more are sensitive to the needs of somone who loses a pet. If your friends, co-workers, or family members are not sympathetic to your loss, it may help to seek out other pet owners, who are more likely to understand your feelings.

Sometimes we think that something must be wrong with us for feeling a powerful loss when a ferret dies. This may be especially true for those of us who have lost a close human loved one. We may feel that the grief over losing a pet should not be as great as the grief over losing a person. But there is nothing rational about our feelings. Often our ferrets have been our closest companions — never fighting with us, always there for us, always dependent upon us for their well-being. Remember that the feelings of loss are normal when a beloved pet dies. Allow yourself time to grieve the loss.

Humans are not the only ones who feel sad when a ferret dies. The other ferrets in the group and even other pets in the home will likely feel a loss. You can help your ferrets and other pets through the grieving process by giving them extra attention. In some cases, a cage-mate might become so depressed that he or she stops eating. You will need to watch for this and take proper steps to help the ferret through (that is, force-feedings if necessary and lots of extra attention). A trip to the veterinarian could be in order.

Dear Gabby

YOUR ADVICE FERRET

NEW FERRET HAZING & DON'T LIKE BATHS

You're staring at me!

Dear Gabby:

I'm the new kid in the family and all my older brothers and sisters are dragging me all over the place. What should I do? — Dragged around in Buffalo

Koosh dragging me around.

Dear Dragged:

Older ferrets often drag us young kits around. That's just a normal part of the ferret hazing ritual. The time-honored rule

Me in my separate cage.

is: No blood, no foul. Of course, that doesn't mean you can't scream your head off. (How do you think I got the name Gabby?) Eventually you'll learn how to handle yourself (at which point you'll be ready to bully whatever new kits come on the scene). My humans kept me in a separate cage when I was really small and supervised my interactions with the older ferrets until they were sure I was able to take care of myself. The small separate cage also makes it easier for us to learn proper litter box usage.

Dear Gabby:

I don't like baths! HELP!
— Stinky in Tallahassee

Dear Stinky:

Take heart and remember that ferrets don't need to be bathed all that often! Your sleeping cloths

HA! HA! Koosh getting a bath!

and hammocks should get washed a lot more often than you do. If your humans keep your cage clean and your ears clean (not that that's fun!), you should generally be able to go for a while without a bath (unless you keep up that nasty habit of rolling in the dust behind the couch!). Of course, once in a while, baths happen.

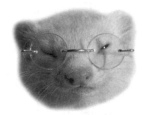

Marshmallow Explains It All™

GETTING A LEG UP WITH HUMANS

I have become gleefully aware of the ease with which one of the ferret persuasion — such as myself — can take shameless advantage of one of the human persuasion — such as my moderately hairless friend and slave Eric the Human.

I have heard humans ask one another with regard to us fur-bearing quadrupeds: "Do you think they know they're cute?" Of course we *know* we're cute. However, these humans assume it is a silly question and that we ferrets could not possibly realize the scope of our adorableness. This is why we are superior, my friends. Our cuteness affords us the ability to take complete and easy advantage of the opposable thumbs that are attached to these easily swayed two-legged creatures. That is the key, of course — the thumbs. We ferrets do not have them, though we would put them to far better use than any of those two-legged types do. Indeed, opposable thumbs are wasted on humans. But that doesn't mean we cannot have full and free use of the thumbs by way of subtle manipulation.

Case in point: I have been suffering for the past several months with spells of low blood sugar caused by insulinoma. I cannot have surgery for the insulinoma (a debulking or a partial pancreatectomy) because of the extensive surgery my doctor had to perform to remove an ugly adrenal growth from my vena cava. But that is Ferretone out of the bottle. My humans have decided to stay an increase in the dose of prednisone I receive every day by ensuring that I eat several times a day. (This is an excellent way to help your ferret with insulinoma — frequent high-protein snacks to supplement his regular diet.) Eric the Human has taken on the task of crushing food and wetting it down for me (I will enlighten my readers with training techniques at a later date). He then sets me on the table with a bowl in front of me. Here is the part I love: As I lap up the mush, Eric turns the bowl so that I do not have to stretch to reach the food. To me, this is a wonderful use of the opposable thumbs. Next I shall see if I can get him to wipe my face for me. After that … the sky's the limit! Ah, me, how particularly trainable humans can be (sigh).

Providing an insulinomic ferret with frequent, nutritious, high-protein meals can help him maintain a more regular blood sugar level and enable him to live longer with a higher quality of life. Ferrets with insulinoma often seem to forget to eat frequently enough on their own, which is why it is important for you to feed them.

Sabrina Says:™

THOSE DANGEROUS HOLIDAYS

We're at the time of year when everyone is having a celebration for one holiday or another: Thanksgiving, Christmas, Hanukkah, Kwanza, New Year's. When you make up your invitation lists for your cocktail and dinner parties, think about your most special guests — your ferrets. Do you really want them dancing with Aunt Sally in her spiked heels or eating cocktail wieners with Uncle Sid?

Your ferrets are the last ones to begrudge you a joyous celebration, but they will appreciate it if you take the time to think about their safety before you put on that lampshade and do the hula on the coffee table.

Things To Watch Out For

Ferrets are curious. When new things (like presents or wrapping supplies) or people (like visitors) show up in your home, your ferrets need to investigate. It is a fact of ferret life that no matter how intelligent we are, if something seems interesting, we might eat it. One of the major causes of ferret illness and death is intestinal blockage. To avoid having your fuzzy spend the holidays at the veterinarian's, take the time to keep hazardous materials out of ferret reach.

Some foods can also cause intestinal blockages. Other foods can cause diarrhea or other gastrointestinal upsets. Make sure you tell your guests that they shouldn't feed the ferrets anything but ferret-designated treats. Explain that ferrets cannot eat all sorts of table foods. In general don't give these foods to your ferrets:

- Nuts
- Alcoholic beverages
- Dairy foods
- Candy
- Overly salty foods (chips)
- Foods containing high amounts of sugar

People To Watch Out For

Once you've taken everything hazardous out of your ferrets' reach, consider your guests. Usually, the best thing to do when you have guests into your home is to keep the ferrets in a secure place (usually their cage). You can always let them exercise before your guests arrive. Depending on the type of people you will be entertaining (wild and crazy or sedate and reserved), you may want to keep the ferrets in an out-of-the-way place like a bedroom (for their own safety) or in their cage out in plain view (so they can see what's going on and you can supervise your guests' interaction with them). You can bring your ferrets out and introduce them to your guests, but be cautious about leaving the ferrets out while others are in your home. Unless your guests are used to having fuzzies underfoot, you'll want to keep your ferrets caged to prevent any accidents. In addition to intestinal blockages, crushing accidents are a major cause of ferret death and injury in the home. Guests in the throes of celebration might not keep an eye out for your ferrets like you do.

Make sure you tell your guests what the house rules are regarding the ferrets. If you have children visiting your home, don't assume their parents will tell them how to behave with your ferrets. If they are very young children who are not used to ferrets, consider locking the ferrets in a room while your guests are visiting. If the children are good with pets, you may want to allow them some supervised time with your ferrets. Remember, your ferrets depend on you to keep them safe, so keep them away from people (adults or children) who you know will not handle them properly.

Be Prepared For Emergencies

In case there is an accident, make sure you have the number of a 24-hour emergency veterinary clinic on hand. Talk to your veterinarian *now* so you will have the information if and when you need it. Also keep the number of the National Animal Poison Control Center by your telephone. This is a non-profit organization that provides around-the-clock service by veterinarians. Here are the phone numbers:

National Animal Poison Control Center

1-900-680-0000 — $20.00 for the first 5 minutes, plus $2.95 for each additional minute

1-800-548-2423 — $30.00 per case, credit cards only

Ferret Toy Do's and Don'ts

If you are getting your ferret a gift this holiday season, remember that not all toys that say they are for ferrets are safe for ferrets. Think about the toys before you buy them. Are they sturdy? Can pieces be torn off and swallowed? Will you have to supervise your ferret while he plays with it? Always remember to check toys periodically for wear and tear.

Instead of getting toys for your ferret, think about getting him something more practical (since most prefer playing with a crumpled piece of paper or a stolen stinky sock anyway). Of course, if you're creative, you could always make something for your ferrets.

Most of all, remember to make time for your ferrets during this busy season. Between shopping and entertaining and visiting friends and family, the little guys can sometimes begin to feel a little left out. Make sure you take a ferret break — it will let them know you love them and it'll give you that little lift you've been looking for.

Here are some of the things you'll want to keep out of ferret reach:
Ribbon/bows
Tinsel, garland, tree ornaments
Christmas lights/wires
Menorahs/candles (especially when lit)
Decorations they might chew on
Box packing material (foam peanuts, plastic "grass")
Rubber bands
Styrofoam
Wrapping paper/tissue paper
Pins from new clothing (straight pins)
Plastic price tag fasteners on clothing
Children's toys (dolls, doll shoes & purses)
Christmas tree/plants (e.g., poinsettia)

DON'TS
Anything made of soft rubber or latex
Foam toys
Easily torn toys
Toys that can be swallowed

DO'S
Hammock or sleeping sack (but watch out for beds with exposed foam rubber)
Food dish or water bottle
Leash or harness
Cage or travel cage (pet taxi)
New (sharper) nail clippers

Trixie's Tips™

My tips!

EXTRA LITTER BOXES!

A lot of humans think cleaning litter boxes is a pain in the tail. Daily scooping is hard enough, but that weekly scouring can be *work*. But you have to do it because we ferrets don't like to have to use a dirty toilet (I bet you don't either). Besides, dirty litter boxes can make ferrets and humans sick. And they stink (we've got delicate little noses, y'know). But if you have a whole extra set of litter boxes, then you don't have to rush around trying to clean them, dry them, and re-fill them while we ferrets are waiting to get our toilet back. Instead, you can fill the new set of litter boxes with clean litter and put them in the place of the dirty ones. Then you can wash and dry the dirty litter boxes whenever you want (sooner is better than later, if you want my opinion). Switching in all new litter boxes in a ferret's cage goes really fast, so the ferret hardly notices. Make sure you have a replacement box for every litter box in your house (we have a bunch in our cage and a couple around our room).

When you're washing the litter boxes, you can use antibacterial hand soap or antibacterial dishwashing liquid. A lot of humans mix together a solution of water and bleach. If you use bleach, make sure you rinse and rinse and rinse! Then it's a good idea to let the boxes dry in the sun. If your litter boxes get stains that won't come out, you probably want to go buy new boxes. Our humans found litter boxes that have a slick coating on the inside so that stuff can't get absorbed into the plastic so easily.

If you are pregnant, it's a good idea to give up the litter box chores to someone else in the family. Although ferrets do not usually engage in behaviors that expose them to toxoplasmosis (that is, digging in the dirt outside), they can get it. If you have cats in your home that go outside and they share a litter box with your ferrets, then your ferrets could be exposed. (Cats are the more common source of toxoplasmosis.) Although toxoplasmosis is a serious concern for pregnant women, there is no need to get rid of your pets. Avoiding litter box scooping and cleaning is the usual recommendation. Even if you do not have cats and your ferrets do not go outside, it's better to err on the safe side and give the litter box duties to someone else. If you have concerns or questions about toxoplasmosis, talk to your obstetrician/gynecologist. Your doctor can perform a test to see if you have ever been exposed to toxoplasmosis (if you've had cats that go outdoors, you've most likely been exposed) and advise you further.

Marshmallow Explains It All™

THE SCENT OF A FERRET (HOO HA!)

I am often invited to move among some very sophisticated human social circles. Humans find me utterly charming (which, of course, I am), and I am considered among the most desirable guests to be seated next to at a dinner party. Because of my erudite commentary on all things ferret, I am looked up to — despite my diminutive stature — by scores of humans who cling to my every syllable.

During my jaunts into the world of human culture, I pay scrupulous attention to the conversations going on around me. For I am a scholar of not only ferret but also human nature. I wouldn't exactly call it eavesdropping, but someone less well-bred might.

At a recent soiree, I had the pleasure of listening in on a particularly absorbing discourse about the scents of various ferrets. I was astonished. Could humans truly recognize the exquisite complexity of the nuance-rich aromatic language of the mustelid? I turned a particularly keen ear and learned that humans *can* differentiate among ferrets based on the ferret's fragrance. However, it was only the considerably concentrated sleep aroma that the humans were able to recognize. Still, I was impressed with this ability that I had heretofore believed was beyond the modest olfactory purview of humans.

Perhaps you human readers have also noticed the broad array of alluring scents that arise from the lithe bodies of sleeping ferrets. Like people, ferrets each have a unique bouquet. Even the most smelling challenged of humans can sniff a sleeping ferret and recognize that different ferrets have different scents.

Some of the various aromas that humans have identified as being emitted by their ferrets are corn chips, popcorn, musk (like the cologne), grape soda, and "ew!" The last so-called fragrance being strong evidence of the impudent lack of appreciation humans have for the elegance of the ferret perfume (and may simply be an indication that the human has been remiss in cleaning the ferret's ears).

The various limbs of a ferret may issue varied smells. Let us consider Bosco da Gama, for example. A warm musky aroma emanates from Bosco's head, but his tail smells like grape soda. The grape soda phenomenon is a mystery even to me (so you humans should abandon any hope of comprehending its origin).

I, on the other paw, take on an all-over popcorn aroma when I sleep, as does Sabrina. Knuks smells more like a warm corn chip or tortilla. Cauliflower takes on strong hob-like fragrance, despite his being a gib. These are but a few examples.

Of course, ferret scents are even more intricate than what I have outlined here. They possess subtle differences that humans could not expect to discern but that we ferrets find to be obvious. Despite your human shortcomings, I would like to suggest you take a moment to identify the aroma your ferrets emit when they sleep. It is the first step towards a better understanding and closer bond between you and your master, the ferret.

Sabrina Says:™

HOW TO GIVE BAD-TASTING MEDICINE

Note: This is a feeding syringe (no needle) used to accurately measure the amount of medicine. Since Sabrina likes the taste, she is lapping from the syringe, thus there is no need to try to get the medicine between her cheek and gums. If she didn't like the taste, we would have put the syringe tip in from the side of her mouth to put the medicine in the center of her mouth (not into the back of her throat).

Sick ferrets are often still strong enough to push away bad-tasting medicine. To get the medicine into the ferret, scruff him to keep him still. If this doesn't work, wrap the ferret in a towel while scruffing him to keep his front feet from reaching his mouth. The towel should be snug near the neck and looser around the rest of the body. Be careful not to wrap too tightly. Now you can get the medicine to your ferret's lips without him pawing your hand away.

Never put medicine into the back of your ferret's throat — he will choke. Lift the ferret's lip and dribble the medicine between the cheek and gums. Another trick is to put a drop of Ferretone or other lickable treat (Nutri-Cal, Ferretvite) on the ferret's nose and, as he begins to lick, dribble the medicine onto the tip of his tongue. (Thanks to Dr. Michael Dutton for his help.)

Ask you veterinarian to demonstrate if necessary.

MORTAR AND PESTLE!

You can use a mortar and pestle (available at a housewares store) to grind up and crush your ferret's dry food into a fine powder. This will make it easier to add water and make a smooth mush. Sometimes a mush like this is all that a sick ferret is willing to eat.

You can help your ferret get used to this kind of mush by taking the little crunched bits left over in the food bowl and wetting them down as an occasional treat. Remember that getting your ferret used to a food like this when he is healthy will make it easier to feed him mush when he is sick.

Marshmallow Explains It All™

CREATIVE THINKING

The common housecat or the faithful hound has its attractive attributes that lure humans into its furry clutches. However, it is only the ferret that presents the intellectual challenge upon which discriminating humans truly thrive.

Dogs follow directions. They are exceedingly good at doing so, and should be commended with a heart-felt pat on the head and a good scratching behind the ears or on the belly. Cats behave like actors upon a stage and their enthralling performances deserve copious recompense with fishy treats and saucers of milk (or non-dairy alternative). But ferrets are different — and, dare I say, superior? — animals.

We earn our keep (raisins aplenty and free-flowing Ferretone) by providing our humans constant mental stimulation. Our minds are always seeking the new; this is what you humans call "curiosity." By flexing our ever-agile cerebral matter, we discover and devise means to attain our goals — be those goals reaching the top of a bookcase where treats are cached, purloining fragrant socks and secreting them beneath the couch, or discovering a route to the desk where the "no-no's" are kept.

Inventiveness was a key component to our wild ancestors' survival as a solitary animal in need of food and shelter. As a solitary hunter, the polecat needed to ferret out food on his own (whereas dogs follow the leader of the pack). This problem-solving ability is one of the attributes we polecat progeny have retained throughout the domestication process.

In practical terms, what this means to the humans who provide for us is that we are in constant need of protection from Trouble. Well, humans call it Trouble; we ferrets call it our manifest destiny. Humans must regularly review the ferret environment for potential dangers that we will invariably discover; in brief, ferret-proofing is an ongoing responsibility. As humans rearrange our environments to make them safer, we are intellectually obligated to pursue other avenues towards our destiny (humans read: Trouble). But this curiosity is what makes us ferrets the exemplary companions that we are. Without our creative thinking, we would be banal lumps of fur slinking about your living room. There is no glory in that.

Therefore, let dogs keep their best-friend status — we ferrets prefer to be adulated for our creative thinking, our quick wit, and our clever discourse.

To help prevent your ferret from getting bored and engaging in destructive behaviors, provide new toys and rotate the toys periodically. Rotating the toys means taking away toys that your ferret no longer plays with and replacing them with other toys. When the excitement of the "new" toys wears off, rotate them out and bring back the old toys, which will now seem "new" again. The ferret's creative mind needs entertainment and stimulation.

Sabrina Says:™

IF YOU CAN'T STAND THE HEAT...

The weather is warming up and summer is not far behind. For many people that means spending more time outdoors. It also means that people want to bring their ferrets with them to visit places like parks or other people's homes. The most important thing to remember is that ferrets cannot tolerate high temperatures. You must take precautions so that your ferrets are protected from the heat if you must transport them in the warm weather. It helps to follow some sensible guidelines.

Never leave your ferret in a parked car in the warm weather. Not even for a minute. Not even if it isn't *hot* outside. The temperature in a closed car increases faster than you might think. Your ferret can get heatstroke and die within only a few minutes. If you can't take your ferret inside with you wherever you're going, leave him home. (This should actually be written in stone.)

Never leave your ferret in direct sunlight. If your ferret's cage is near a window, make sure he has access to a cool, shaded area within his cage. Better still, move the cage away from the window, especially during the warmer months. If your home is not air conditioned, make sure your ferrets are kept in the coolest place possible in your house. You might want to fill an empty milk container or other re-sealable container with water and freeze it. Wrap the container in a towel and put it in the cage or carrier (if you're transporting the ferret in a car without A/C) with the ferret, this will help keep the ferret cool.

As a rule, if it's over 80 to 85 degrees* outside, leave your fuzzies at home unless they *have* to go somewhere (like to the veterinarian).

If the temperature is lower than 80 to 85 degrees and you want to take your fuzzy out for a walk or to visit, try to follow these suggestions. Avoid going out during the hottest times of the day (10 am to 2 pm in the Northeast). Bring cool water for your ferret to drink. Watch your ferret closely for any signs of heatstroke. If you notice any of these signs, get your ferret out of the heat immediately. Seek veterinary attention if the symptoms don't improve within a few minutes. Signs of heatstroke include open-mouth breathing or panting, "flat-ferret," limpness, disorientation, unconsciousness.

If you think your ferret is suffering from heatstroke, cool him off. You can do this by submerging the paws in *cool* (not cold) water and/or placing a cool damp cloth on the ferret's paws/legs. Do not force fluids into your ferret. Offer him water. Do not delay in getting him to the vet, particularly if he has any of the more severe signs of heatstroke (loss of consciousness, disorientation) or if he refuses to take water. He may need subcutaneous fluids or other treatment.

Sometimes what's fun for you isn't very fun for your ferret. Following simple, common sense guidelines when you take your ferret outdoors in the warm weather will ensure that you avoid any tragedies.

Some experts say 80 degrees, some say 90 degrees. Certainly different ferrets may have difficulty at differing temperatures over 80 degrees (some will be fine until 90 degrees, others will be intolerant of anything over 80 degrees). Watch your ferrets closely.

My tips!

Trixie's Tips™

KAO LECTROLYTE
(ELECTROLYTE REPLENISHER)

Ferrets are little animals, so when they don't feel well they need attention right away, especially if they're vomiting or have diarrhea. Dehydration can happen fast — particularly during the summer. But sometimes giving plain water isn't enough, the ferret needs to have his electrolytes replaced. Veterinarians recommend Pedialyte (or generic) or Gatorade (or other electrolyte-replacing sports drink). Our humans found Kao Lectrolyte, an electrolyte replacer that comes in powder form and can be mixed one cup at a time. This is particularly helpful with ferrets, since the liquid form usually comes in quart size (some brands are available in smaller sizes) and cannot be stored for more than 48 hours once you open it (unless you freeze it). A quart is more than you will use in that amount of time. These little packets can be stored easily, without taking up very much space. You can find electrolyte replacers in the baby products aisle at the supermarket or sometimes next to the diarrhea medicines. Keep some in your home for emergencies.

Kao Lectrolyte is an electrolyte replacer that comes in convenient powder packets — so you can always have some on hand in case of emergency.

Some ferret owners give an electrolyte replacer regularly during the summer as a precaution against dehydration.

If you can't find Kao-Lectrolyte or Pedialyte, you can give a dehydrated ferret Gatorade or other sports drink that replaces potassium and sodium.

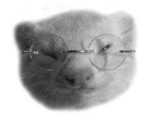

Marshmallow Explains It All™

THE LITTER BOX JITTER BUG
(AND RELATED DANCE STEPS)

We ferrets can be a bit fussy about things from time to time. Take the litter box. I like my litter boxes fairly clean (most ferrets do). Usually I have to check and double check — even triple check — that I've got the right spot to "go" in. Sometimes I can't even decide if I have to go to the bathroom or if I came into the cage to get a bite to eat or have a sip of water. I get a little distracted. Other ferrets get the urge to "go" and head straight for the litter box, jump in, and do their thing. No hemming or hawing. Either of these behaviors is pretty normal. It's only if you see your ferret trying to "go" and nothing comes out that you have to take him to the vet.

Now, I'm a long fellow. I like to have all four feet in the litter box. If you give me a short litter box, I'll go near it, but not in it. No offense, but I'm a little particular. If I absolutely have to, I'll rest my front feet on the edge of the litter box so I can make a deposit in the proper spot.

Although most of us prefer a little privacy while we're doing our thing in the litter box, sometimes our humans watch us to make sure we're OK (of course, whenever I try to do that to them, I get shooed away). This is when they notice that we go into a sort of trance while we're actually "going." Those humans that are unfamiliar with the Litter Box Trance become concerned that we're sick or something. We're not. We just have to think hard to get it right. No, not really. That's a joke. The point is that we're not sick, we're just ignoring you.

Another one of the normal behaviors that humans get concerned about is — how shall I put this? — "cleanliness." After I use the litter box, I usually wipe my rear on the towel or floor next to the litter box. I've heard that when canines or felines do this it means they're sick. Well, when we ferrets do it, we're being clean*. I think that this behavior proves that we are much more closely related to humans — who also display this type of behavior — than dogs or cats. Now, which kind of animal would you want to share *your* raisins with?

If your ferret suddenly becomes fussy about the litter box, watch to see if he is having difficulty urinating or defecating. Difficulty urinating or defecating can be a sign of a serious medical problem and should be brought to your veterinarian's attention.

* Even though most pet ferrets have been descented (the anal scent gland has been removed), they still behave as if the gland were there. Rubbing their behinds after defecating is a way of communicating with other ferrets through smell (aka marking).

DISTRACTING YOUR FERRET
WITH LICKABLE TREATS

If your ferret makes a fuss when you try to clip her nails, try using an oil-based coat supplement (Ferretone, FuroTone, Linatone) or other "lickable" substance to distract your ferret. You can use this same method to distract your ferret when she's getting a shot or any other time you need to keep your ferret occupied.

For nail clipping, put a few drops of the oily supplement on the belly and show your ferret where it is. The ferret is usually so wrapped up in licking that she doesn't notice her nails are being clipped. Or, instead of putting it on the ferret's belly, you can put your ferret on a countertop and put a few drops on a spoon in front of her. At the vet's office, a few drops of the oily supplement or a small blob of vitamin supplement paste (Ferretvite, FuroVite, Nutri-Cal) can keep your ferret distracted while the vet gives a shot or performs an examination.

It works!

Most ferrets are very distracted by licking a treat off their bellies. This gives you an opportunity to clip their nails or examine them without them getting wiggly. You may have to help by pointing their nose towards the treat. Note: Some ferrets may tickle themselves when they start licking!

Marshmallow Explains It All™

DON'T BE BLUE... IT'S FUR THE BEST

Humans have a tendency to get worked up over their ferrets. It's all right; we sort of like the attention. Although the constant ear-checking and poop-inspecting can become a tad tiresome. Whenever we try to look into our humans' ears, we're greeted with shrieks. Forget about letting us anywhere near their litter box. Well, never mind.

One of the things humans often become concerned over are strange markings on our skin. Some of the markings are tattoos from the breeder where we were born. Others aren't markings at all.

Take the shaved ferret, for example. The ferret has been through some sort of surgery and has come out all right. Either the stitches have been taken out or they were the type which dissolve over time. The ferret is feeling full of vim and vigor. Then comes the human's most disturbing observation that the ferret's skin has turned blue — or a purplish blue or a bluish purple. Sometimes the human imagines internal bruising and other horrific post-surgical complications. A frantic phone call to the veterinarian does not always produce a satisfactory explanation.

Don't panic. It's only fur.

That's right. Often, the dark tips of the ferret's new guard hairs cause the skin to take on a bluish tint as they appear just beneath the skin's surface. Given a few more days or so, you will see the peach-fuzz–like growth of new fur. Of course, if your ferret is pale, like I am, you might see a grayish tint to the skin prior to the appearance of new fur growth.

Once the ferret's new fur has grown in, don't be surprised if the color of the newly grown patch of fur is different from that of the rest of the ferret's fur. Ferrets shed twice yearly, and the texture and color of their coats (and masks) can change sometimes dramatically during these seasonal transformations. Thus, it is normal for the next season's fur to grow in to replace the fur that has been shaved off. Humans may find the color variation more pronounced in ferrets whose coat color and markings change a good deal from season to season. Oddly enough, this phenomenon apparently occurs in other species, like dogs and cats. I suspect they're copying us, since ferrets are, by far, much better and more brilliant than any other animal in the universe. Besides, why do you think they call them copyCATS?

Until next time, adieu.

When a ferret has undergone surgery, he often has bruises around the area of the incision. These bruises will heal with time (usually a few days). If the bruises get worse or fade and then come back, or if your ferret seems sore or lethargic, bring it to your veterinarian's attention.

Remember that undergoing surgery is physically draining for a ferret (just as it is for a person), and he will need time and rest in order to recuperate. Make sure that your recovering ferret is eating and drinking sufficiently and is urinating and defecating normally.

Some ferret breeders that sell to pet stores mark their ferrets with small tattoos on the ears or toes. These are usually fairly easy to discern from bruises.

Sabrina Says:™

GET A SECOND MEDICAL OPINION

Sometimes a ferret is sick with something mysterious and the ferret's regular veterinarian doesn't know what to make of it. When this kind of thing happens with people, you go to another doctor to get a second opinion. There are situations wherein you need to take your ferret for a second opinion, too. Sometimes your current veterinarian may not be totally up-to-date on ferrets, and sometimes it's just a very tricky problem to diagnose.

We have gotten phone calls and e-mails from people asking us what we think is wrong with their ferret. Since we are not veterinarians, it is often very difficult to even make a suggestion about what could be wrong with the ferret. There are times when we can help because the ferret has symptoms that are obviously associated with a very common type of problem (for example, baldness with adrenal disease or projectile vomiting with a complete intestinal blockage). But we prefer to leave medical topics to the professionals (veterinarians).

So if your ferret is sick and your veterinarian doesn't know what's wrong, try going to another doctor to get a second opinion. It doesn't mean you have to change veterinarians permanently. But it is important to get the ferret to someone who can help him. Your own veterinarian might even recommend another veterinarian you can go to. Remember that not all veterinarians know about ferrets. One of the most important things you can do for your ferret is to find a ferret-knowledgeable veterinarian.

Not all medical problems occur during office hours. Talk with your regular veterinarian about where you should go if you have a ferret medical emergency. Not all emergency veterinary clinics will see ferrets. Some emergency clinics that do see ferrets may know only the basics. Find an emergency veterinary clinic you can trust *before* you need one. Always follow up with your regular veterinarian after an emergency veterinarian visit.

Marshmallow Explains It All™

IF FERRETS AREN'T RODENTS, WHY DO THEY GET RAT TAIL?

I have been the honored recipient of several communiqués inquiring about the worrisome subject of tail-tip baldness, also known as (shudder) "Rat Tail." Mind you, I'm speaking of hair loss that begins at the *tip* of the tail, not the base of the tail (near the buttocks). Hair loss at the base of the tail is another matter entirely, and requires veterinary attention, as it is likely a sign of a problem with the adrenal glands.

Despite vicious rumors to the contrary, we ferrets are, for the most part, impeccable about our grooming. Of course, there is the occasional derelict who rolls in the litter box, but most of us are above such contemptible behavior. However, despite our fastidious primping, some of us ferrets end up with Rat Tail. Rat Tail is a condition wherein the tail becomes bald or near-bald, and thus takes on the loathsome appearance of the tail of a rat. Of course, ferrets are not rats and, therefore, some of us find such a comparison to be frightfully disturbing (though the social ramifications of such a likening escape the more common ferret). Through no fault of our own, we ferrets have many sebaceous (oil) glands all over our skin. The oil helps us maintain our magnificently soft, sleek coats. Unfortunately, too much of the oil can lead to a build-up on the skin, which leads to blocked pores, blackheads, and hair loss — the hallmarks of Rat Tail. But fear not fair ferrets! Rat Tail can be treated.

Compassionate humans who wish to appropriately serve their ferret masters can take steps to eradicate Rat Tail. At the first signs of oily build-up (blackheads, reddish crusting), begin to cleanse the ferret's tail regularly using a few drops of ferret shampoo (some available ferret shampoos are formulated to help dissolve the oil). Alternatively, humans may use a mild (and I mean *mild!*) acne-type cleanser made for humans (our human uses a Neutrogena product on Cauliflower's tail). Be sure to *completely* rinse the product from the ferret's tail. If you are attentive to your ferret's cleansing needs, you will be able to treat and prevent the heartbreak of Rat Tail. Your ferret will be grateful, especially if you also give him a raisin to help ease his anguish.

Hair loss that begins at the base of the tail and progresses up the body is a sign of adrenal disease. Sometimes the hair loss begins on the top of the tail, other times it begins underneath the tail. See your veterinarian about hair loss at the base of the tail or any of these other symptoms: hair loss on the hind end, shoulders, or tops of feet; a swollen vulva in females or sexual (mounting) behavior in males; aggression, straining to urinate, lethargy (sleepiness), muscle loss, itchy skin, or shiny, scaly appearing skin. These are symptoms of adrenal disease, which needs to be treated by your veterinarian.

Sabrina Says:™

GIVE A KIT A SMELLY T-SHIRT

Humans like to bond with their new ferrets (and ferrets like to bond with humans, too). One of the best ways to get your new ferret to bond with you is to appeal to the ferret's sense of smell. A ferret's sense of smell is his keenest sense. To get a baby ferret (kit) used to your particular aroma, give him an old T-shirt (or sweatshirt) to sleep in. You should wear the T-shirt first, so it has your scent on it. This way, the kit is getting used to your smell even when you're not holding him. This will also help to make your ferret happier when you do hold him because you smell like something familiar to him.

Good luck with your new addition!

Koosh sleeping with one of Eric's T-Shirts.

APPENDIX

TEN TIPS FOR NEW FERRET OWNERS

1. Find a good veterinarian

A good ferret veterinarian is important for helping you keep your ferret healthy throughout his life. Ferrets require annual vaccinations against rabies and canine distemper. A new ferret should always be brought to a veterinarian for a checkup (your vet may want you to bring a stool sample). At that time you can discuss your ferret's vaccination schedule (baby ferrets require a series of vaccinations in order to be properly protected against distemper). Your veterinarian can demonstrate proper ear cleaning, nail clipping, and dental hygiene techniques.

2. Food and treats

Many high-quality ferret foods are now available. Remember that better nutrition will help your ferret have a longer and healthier life. Ferrets are carnivores, and their food should have meat as its main ingredient(s). We recommend offering multiple brands of food, especially for young ferrets (ferrets imprint on food very young and can be finicky eaters as adults), to help them learn to enjoy different foods (in case for some reason you are no longer able to get a certain brand). Offer food and water at all times. Very young ferrets need their food wet down for them until their teeth and jaws are ready for hard food. Treats are not a substitute for good food. Ferrets crave attention and will often even enjoy their regular food as a treat if you give it to them by hand.

3. Litter-box training

Ferrets can be trained to use litter boxes, providing that you put in the effort. Ferrets naturally like to go in the same spot they went before, they prefer to back into corners, and they like to avoid going places where they eat, drink, sleep, or play. You can encourage good litter box use by (1) providing enough litter boxes in their cage and in the rooms that they play in (ferrets don't generally want to go too far once they decide the need a litter box) and (2) discouraging them from going in "wrong" places by putting down food bowls, sleeping blankets, or toys. Start by allowing your ferret in a small area with a litter box and expand your ferret's roaming area as he displays good litter box use.

4. Grooming

Ferrets are basically clean creatures, but they do require some grooming help. They require regular ear cleaning and nail clipping. Ferret-specific ear cleaning solutions are available. Nail clipping can be done much more easily if you distract the ferret (placing a lickable treat on the belly works wonders — clip the nails while he licks it off). Ferrets can be bathed when they get dirty; however, bathing too frequently will only cause them to produce more of their natural oils (which will make them smell muskier). Ferrets shed their coats (and gain or lose weight) twice a year. When your ferret is shedding, administer a hairball remedy to help him pass any fur he swallows.

5. Odor control

Ferrets naturally have a musky ferret smell (which many owners find quite pleasant — if you object to the smell, then ferrets may not be right for you). There are other smells which you will want to reduce. Keeping litter boxes clean (scoop daily and wash regularly) and washing bedding will help reduce odors. Also make sure that the ferret's ears are regularly cleaned (ear wax can smell bad). Ferrets that are not neutered or spayed will smell stronger than those that are (most ferrets sold in pet stores are already altered).

6. Nip training and socializing

Ferrets are social animals; they want to play with you. They are very smart and can learn to play properly if you expect it of them. Ferrets don't have hands, so they use their mouths to grab things. They play with each other by mock combat; you must teach them that playing with humans is not like playing with other ferrets. They will learn this if you are gentle and consistent with teaching them. Mother ferrets grab their kits by the scruff of the neck to discipline them — you can do the same. Do not hit your ferret, but rather work gently with him so that he can understand what you want. Offer lickable treats from your hands so that your ferret learns that licking you is a pleasant experience. Offer your ferret toys to play roughly with if he wants to.

Work with your ferret's natural desires — when he first wakes up he wants to run around and play, when he is tired he wants to curl up and snuggle.

Playing with your ferret and getting him used to having his feet held and teeth examined while he is young will make grooming easier when he is older.

7. Housing

For their protection, we recommend that ferrets be caged when you aren't around to supervise their play (their curiosity can get them into dangerous situations they can't necessarily get out of). Your ferret's cage should be a safe haven, with food, water, litter box(es), and sleeping blankets or hammocks available. Ferrets should have a wire cage (no fish tanks) with a floor covered with material to protect their feet. Since ferrets use a litter box, there is no need for wood chips/shavings in their cage (also, cedar and pine shavings are a health hazard to ferrets) — instead provide bedding blankets made from old sweatshirts, T-shirts, etc.

8. Ferret proofing

Ferrets are very curious and intelligent. They especially like problem solving — which means problem creating for you. They will try to figure out how to climb things, get into things, and get under things. Ferret proofing is the ongoing process of getting down to their level and making sure that there isn't anything harmful or dangerous that they could get into. A common serious ferret problem is intestinal blockage caused by swallowing something that can't fit through their digestive tract. Protect your ferret by monitoring what he is playing with and making sure he isn't accidentally chewing off any pieces.

9. Play and intellectual stimulation

Ferrets are highly intelligent animals that require daily play time and intellectual stimulation. This means that they need exercise and they need you to play with them every day. Ferrets appreciate toys as simple as an empty box or a dangling towel. By providing your ferret with intellectual stimulation you will help prevent him from exhibiting bad behaviors due to stress or boredom. The amount of play a ferret requires depends on his age and health; young ferrets can require several hours a day, as they get older they slow down and don't run around as much.

10. Respect

Ferrets are living creatures. Consider getting a ferret to be like adopting a child. They need to be taught right from wrong, they will make mistakes, they need affection and attention, they feel fear and pain, they want to play, and so much more. If you care for them and appreciate both their good points and their faults, they will be loving and amusing companions that are unlike any other animal.

NOTE: One of the benefits of the growing popularity of ferrets is the proliferation of ferret-specific products. In the past, ferret owners often had to make do with using cat or dog products. The advantage of ferret-specific products is that they come with directions on how to properly use them.

For a downloadable version of this article to hand out, see the *Modern Ferret* website: http://www.modernferret.com

CHECKLIST OF ITEMS
YOU'LL WANT TO HAVE

Cage: When you aren't around to supervise your ferret, the safest place for your ferret is in his cage. The cage should be a place where your ferret feels comfortable and secure. Cages are often placed in a central room so that even when the ferret is in his cage he can still see what's going on and feel part of the family. The cage should allow free air flow (not an aquarium). To protect the ferret's feet, wire cage bottoms are often covered with carpeting or linoleum. If you think you might get more ferrets in the future, plan ahead with a large enough cage.

Hammock: Ferrets have very flexible spines, and many of them like to sleep curled up in a hammock. It is VERY cute.

Bedding: Soft cloths like old T-shirts or sweatshirts make excellent sleeping blankets for ferrets. Washing the bedding regularly will help reduce the ferret musk smell. Do not use wood chips/shavings.

Food: For many years ferrets were fed high-quality kitten foods, but now there are many high-quality ferret foods available. Since ferrets are carnivores, look for a food with meat as its first ingredient(s). Good nutrition promotes good growth and health, so feed the best food you can. Ferrets should be allowed access to food at all times.

Food Bowl: Ferrets are always playing with things. Look for a heavy bowl that will be more difficult for them to move or flip over.

Water Bottle: Ferrets should have access to water at all times. Although many like to lap water from a bowl, many will also spill the water and play with it. A water bottle will ensure that they always have water available.

Litter Box(es): Ferrets should have a litter box in their cage (more than one if the cage size/number of ferrets warrants it). You will also want litter boxes throughout the rooms where your ferret plays.

Litter: Ferrets are low to the ground and have a slick oily coat. Dusty litters and clumping litters can stick to them and cause problems. There are many litters available now made from things like recycled newspaper or compressed plant fibers that are low in dust.

Treats: Remember that treats are just that — small rewards. They should not be a large part of your ferret's diet. However, they are good for bonding with your ferret and rewarding good behavior, learning tricks, etc.

Shampoo: Ferrets can be bathed anywhere from every few weeks to every few months. Bathing helps reduce the musk smell (although an important part of reducing the smell is keeping the ferret's bedding clean and his ears clean). In the past, tearless baby shampoo was often used, but now there are several ferret-specific shampoos available.

Nail Clippers: Ferrets need their nails clipped on a regular basis to prevent foot damage and to prevent them from accidentally scratching you.

Ear Cleaning Solution: Ferrets need their ears cleaned on a regular basis. Ear wax buildup is smelly and can lead to health problems if not cleaned.

Harness & Leash: Ferrets can slip out of a collar, so you'll want a harness that goes around both the neck and front legs.

Carrying Cage: A portable carrier to be used for bringing the ferret to the veterinarian or other outings. Also can serve as a training aid by serving as a "time-out" cage for a misbehaving ferret.

Toys: Ferrets will entertain themselves with anything they can find. Ferret-safe toys don't have parts they could accidentally chew off and swallow. Always monitor all toys for damage — accidentally swallowed pieces of things can lead to intestinal blockages. People are the best toy of all — spend time playing with your ferret!

For a downloadable version of this article to hand out, see the *Modern Ferret* website: http://www.modernferret.com

INDEX

- A -

adrenal disease, 143
autopsy, 112-113

- B -

bathing, 147
    shampoo, 151
    shedding season, 53, 93, 109,
        115, 147
    water temperature, 65
bedding, 150
behavior
    bonding with humans, 144
    chewing electrical cords, 89
    curiosity, 128-129
    ear licking, 57
    getting along, 46-47, 72, 78, 114-
        115
    litter box habits, 134-135
    litter box moving/dumping, 40-
        41, 100-102
    normal, 96-97, 134-135
    polecats, 86-88, 128-129
    shivering, 64-65
Bitter Apple
    electrical cords, 89
blindness, 106-107
books for veterinarians, 90-91
bottle-brush tail, 80-81
bottles, water
    cleaning, 51
    dishes and, 95, 150
bruising, 138-139
brushing, 93, 108-109
"butt dragging," 134-135

- C -

cages, 150
    climbing, 73-75
    equipping, 150-151

isolation, 66-67, 114-115
    travel carrier, 98, 151
canine distemper vaccination, 42-43
"C" clamps on litter box, 100-102
climbing cages, 73-75
colors
    blaze, 92-93
    mask, 92-93
    panda, 92-93
    roaning, 92-93
    growing fur, 138-139
compounding pharmacy, 69
curiosity, 128-129
cysts, 18-19

- D -

Dear Gabby, 20, 44, 78, 114
death
    grief, 113
    post-mortem exam, 112-113
defecating, difficulty (straining), 135
dehydration, 132-133
diarrhea, 22, 132
distemper vaccination, canine, 42-43

- E -

ears
    cleaning, 147, 151
    licking/sucking, 57
    tattoos, 138-139
electrolyte replacer, 132-133
emergencies, 120
escape
    preventing, 62, 77, 82
    from car, 98

- F -

fasting before surgery, 111
Febreze, 26
feeding

carnivore diet, 28, 150
force feeding medicines, 126
hiding food, 86-88
insulinoma, 116-117
kits, 71
mushy food, 127
treats, 29, 104-105, 118-121, 146, 151
water, lapping, 94-95
Ferretone/Furo-Tone/Linatone, 136
ferret proofing, 82-83, 118-121
appliances, 82-83
cage climbing, 73-75
curiosity and, 128-129
electrical cords, 87
escaping, 76, 82
furniture, 32, 82
guests, 62-63, 76, 103, 118-121
outlets, 17
radiators, 60
stepping on ferrets, preventing, 103, 118-121
styrofoam, 48-50
toys, 56, 120, 121
food, 146, 150
hiding, 86-88
inappropriate, 119
kitten, 29
meat, 28-29
mushy, 127
treats, 29, 104-105, 118-121, 146, 151
force-feeding medications, 126
fur
new growth, 138-139
shedding, 52-53, 92-93

- G -

getting along
adults and kits, 72, 114-115
bottle-brush tail, 80-81
boys, 46-47
boys and girls, 78
grooming each other, 57, 93
kits and adults, 72, 114-115

people and ferrets, 140
grooming, 147
bathing, 65, 93, 115, 151
brushing, 93, 108-109
each other, 57, 93
ears, 57, 147, 151
hairball remedy, 52-53, 93, 109, 147
nails, 58-59, 136-137, 151
rat tail, 142-143

- H -

hairball remedy, 52-53, 93, 109, 147
hairballs, 52-53
hammocks, 150
harness and leash, 151
heatstroke, 130-131
symptoms, 131

- I -

illness
dehydration, 132-133
diarrhea, 22, 132
heatstroke, 130-131
insulinoma diet, 104-105, 116-117
mushy food and, 127
recognizing, 96-97
toxoplasmosis, 123
insulinoma, 105, 116-117
intestinal blockage, 22, 48-50, 52-53, 92, 108, 119, 121
hairballs, 52-53
partial, 52-53, 92, 108
integrating new ferrets, 47, 79
isofluorane anesthesia, 111
isolating sick/recovering ferret, 66-67

- K -

Kao-Lectrolyte electrolyte replacer, 132-133
kits
adults and, 114-115

bonding with people, 144
sense of smell, 144
softening food, 71
special care, 70-72
Knuks Makes Mischief, 32, 60, 100,
73

- L -

litter, 151
litter box, 150
behaviors related to, 134-135
cleaning, 122-123
dumping, preventing (Velcro),
40-41
examining the contents of, 22-23
moving, preventing ("C" clamps),
100-102
replacing, 122-123
training, 146-147

- M -

male ferrets
intact vs. neutered, 46-47
Marshmallow Explains It All, 15, 22,
28, 38, 46, 52, 57, 64, 70, 80,
86, 92, 96, 104, 110, 116, 124,
128, 134, 138, 142
mask
shape changes, seasonal, 92-93,
138-139
mast cell tumors, 19, 110-111
medications, 30, 68
Animal Poison Control Center
numbers, 31, 120
dosages, 68
flavors, 68-69
forcing, 126
prescriptions, checking, 54-55

- N -

nail trimming, 58-59, 136-137, 151
National Animal Poison Control
Center phone number, 31, 120

neutering, 47

- O -

odors
Febreze, 26
marking, 38
reducing, 26, 147
recognizing, 144
sleeping, 124-125

- P -

Pedialyte, 132-133
play, 128-129, 148, 149
see also getting along
see also toys
Poison Control Center, National Animal, phone number, 31, 120
post-mortem exams (autopsies), 112-113
problem solving, 128-129

- R -

rabies vaccination, 42-43
rat tail, 142-143
roaning, 92
rotating toys, 83, 85, 129

- S -

Sabrina Says, 18, 24, 27, 30, 40, 48,
54, 58, 66, 76, 82, 89, 94, 98,
106, 112, 118, 126, 130, 140,
144
scent marking, 38
blind ferrets and, 106-107
bonding with people, 144
new, response to, 80-81
sleeping, 124-125
shedding, 52-53, 92-93
bathing, 53, 92-93, 109, 115, 147
brushing, 93, 108-109
hairball remedy, 52-53, 93, 109
shivering, 64-65

skin tumors, 18-19, 110-111
sleep
    deep, 15, 72
    smell during, 124-125
socialization, 20, 147-148
stress
    bottle-brush tail, 80-81
surgery
    bruising after, 138-139
    fasting before, 111
    general anesthesia during, 111
    hair regrowth, 138-139
    intestinal blockage, 22, 48-50, 52-
        53, 92, 108, 119, 121
    isolation after, 66-67
    skin tumors, 18-19, 110-111

- T -

tattoos, 138-139
toxoplasmosis, 123
toys, 151
    balls, 84
    baskets, 24
    cardboard tubes, 56
    eggs, plastic, 27
    Gumabone, 89
    homemade, 85
    pants legs, 37
    rotating, 83, 85, 129
    safety, 83, 119, 121
training
    chewing, discouraging, 89
    litter, 146-147
    nip-training, 20, 147-148
    time-out, 20, 151
    to lap water, 94-95
traveling
    harness and leash, 151
    pet carrier, 98-99, 151
treats, 104-105, 118-121, 146, 151
    fruits and vegetables, 29
    mushy food, 127
Trixie's Tips, 17, 26, 37, 42, 51, 56,
    62, 68, 84, 90, 103, 108, 122,
    127, 132, 136

tumors
    adrenal, 143
    pancreatic (insulinoma), 116-117
    skin, 18-19, 110-111

- U -

urinating, difficulty (straining), 135

- V -

vaccinations, 42-43, 71, 146
    distracting during, 136-137
vaccine reactions, 43
veterinarian
    emergencies, 120
    second opinions, 140-141
    vaccinations, 146
vitamins
    Ferretvite, Furovite, Nutrical,
        136-137
vomiting and dehydration, 132

- W -

water bottles
    cleaning, 51
    dishes and, 95, 150
weight
    gain, seasonal, 44, 92-93
    loss, seasonal, 44, 92-93
wood shavings, 148, 150

Internet Resources:

www.modernferret.com

Find out all the latest information about *Modern Ferret* Magazine — the magazine that's "For ferret owners. By ferret owners.™" Back issue availability, foreign subscription information, what our current projects are, and more.

* FREE DOWNLOADS * of great stuff including:
  • Health Care Worksheets (keep track of your ferret's medical records)
  • Ten Tips For New Ferret Owners (in a distributable flyer format)
  • Ferret Screensavers

www.newferretowner.com

A brand new resource on the web to help new ferret owners learn everything they need to know about their new friends. Come grow with us!

www.newferretowner.com

www.ferretlovers.com

Attention Ferret Lovers!

yourname@ferretlovers.com
free e-mail address

Get a FREE web-based e-mail account at ferretlovers.com!
Show your love of ferrets with an easy-to-remember e-mail address!
Access your e-mail from anywhere in the world with an Internet connection and a web browser!
It's fun! It's free! It's ferrety-licious!

**WWW.FERRETSUNITEDNETWORK.COM
MEMBER SITE**

Sign up today!

MAGAZINE

*For ferret owners.
By ferret owners.™*

Products available:

___ $19.95 Six-issue US subscription

___ $25.00 Back issue GRAB BAG assortment
of 8 randomly selected back issues

___ $12.95 Book: *The Wit and Wisdom of the
Modern Ferrets -* **Makes a great gift!**
___   *Please have Mary & Eric sign my book!*

*All prices include free shipping in the US
NY residents add sales tax to book orders
For orders outside the US see www.modernferret.com
Make checks or money orders payable to Modern Ferret*

Send orders to:
  Modern Ferret
  Dept: WAW
  PO Box 1007
  Smithtown NY 11787

VISA/MC ORDERS:
Phone 631-981-3643
FAX   631-981-3710

Name_____

Address_____

City_____ State____ ZIP_____

Phone Number (in case we have any questions)_____

Card Number_____

Expires_____ Signature_____